Viking Sagas

The Captivating Tale of Ragnar Lothbrok, Ivar the Boneless, Lagertha, and More, in Their Historical Context

Free Bonus from Captivating History
(Available for a Limited time)

Hi History Lovers!

Now you have a chance to join our exclusive history list so you can get your first history ebook for free as well as discounts and a potential to get more history books for free! Simply visit the link below to join.

Captivatinghistory.com/ebook

Also, make sure to follow us on Facebook, Twitter and Youtube by searching for Captivating History.

Contents

Introduction: The Viking Age

The period between the end of the eighth century CE and the middle of the eleventh is often called the "Viking Age" because this is the period in which Scandinavian people expanded their contacts with the outside world through trade, raiding, exploration, and colonization. This expansion was driven by improvements in shipbuilding technology combined with a culture that valued personal reputation, courage, and martial skill as essential components of one's character, at least for the male portion of the population.

Archaeological evidence can tell us much about how early Scandinavian people lived and died, but it can only take us so far. It is not until the Viking Age that we begin to have enough written evidence to reconstruct aspects of early Scandinavian history and culture. Writing other than runes, which were used for magical and religious purposes, for monuments, or for identifying possessions, was unknown in Scandinavia until the advent of Christianity, which began with Anglo-Saxon missionary efforts in the early eighth century and had taken hold throughout Scandinavia by the twelfth century. The earliest Scandinavian documents, therefore, date from the twelfth century, the period during which Christianity became widespread.

The limited contacts between Scandinavia and more southerly countries all changed in the late eighth century, and the shift is usually dated to the sudden increase in large-scale Viking raids on important religious and political centers, such as the monasteries of Lindisfarne in England in 793 and Iona in Scotland in 795. Incursions into Frankish territory, part of which encompassed areas in what are now France, Germany, and the Low Countries, followed in 799. Further attacks on cities in England and the Frankish Empire increased throughout the ninth century, including the sack of Paris in 845 by a Viking named Ragnar (who may or may not have been the Lothbrok of the saga) and the invasion of England by the so-called "Great Army" in 879.

Most often we know of these attacks not from the perspective of the Vikings themselves but rather from the point of view of their victims and the later medieval historians who recorded what they knew or had been able to learn of these events. Medieval chronicles, usually compiled by clergy in the Frankish Empire or in England, are important primary sources for the activities of Vikings at this time, and it is this view of Vikings as intrepid explorers and vicious plunderers that is at the core of modern popular conceptions about medieval Scandinavian culture.

However, the Viking Age was about much more than longships full of fierce warriors sailing across the seas and down rivers in order to pillage whatever and slay whomever they came across. Medieval Scandinavians also led complex lives that revolved around agriculture, artisanal crafts, and trade, none of which is as exciting to the imagination as a warrior's raid but which stood at the vital economic center of medieval Scandinavian life.

One important product of medieval Scandinavian culture is the corpus of sagas and poetry that first began to be recorded in writing in the twelfth century, although much of that corpus was composed significantly earlier and handed down through oral tradition. The *Saga of Ragnar Lothbrok* is one of these products, combining what may be a grain or two of historical fact with some fairy-tale episodes, connections to other aspects of Norse mythology, and a good helping of Viking derring-do.

This volume presents a version of Ragnar's saga compiled from different modern sources, along with information providing additional historical and documentary context, followed by a discussion of some aspects of modern appropriations and representations of ancient Norse culture. The first section of the book provides historical context for Ragnar's saga through an exploration of daily life in ninth-century Scandinavia and of contemporary Viking culture and history. The text of the saga itself forms the second part of the book, along with notes giving further information about how this version of the saga is presented and about elements within the story that might not be familiar to modern readers. The third section of the book deals with representations of ancient Norse cultures in modern popular media. Because this last topic is too large and too complex to be thoroughly explored in this current volume, I will focus on two areas: dragons in the writings of J. R. R. Tolkien and the conflicts between drama and history in the recent television miniseries, *Vikings*, which itself is based, in part, on the *Saga of Ragnar Lothbrok* and the *Tale of Ragnar's Sons*. And because the *Saga of Ragnar Lothbrok* has important connections to another Icelandic saga, the *Saga of the Volsungs*, a synopsis of *Volsungs* is provided in an appendix.

The Viking Age is a historical period rich with art, poetry, literature, trade, exploration, and battles. The *Saga of Ragnar Lothbrok* is a product of that time and presents to us a story of Vikings not only as they actually may have been, at least in part, but also as they wished to be seen and remembered by later generations. And we still do remember them, over a thousand years after they sailed in search of plunder, trade, and new lands.

Part I: The World of Ragnar Lothbrok

Life in Medieval Scandinavia

Farms and Dwellings

While the modern imagination is full of images of helmeted Vikings jumping out of longships brandishing swords, actual medieval Scandinavian life was rather more prosaic for the majority of the population. Agriculture, animal husbandry, and exploitation of wild food sources such as fish, game, and berries were vital to survival and were widely practiced throughout Scandinavian lands, with certain variations depending upon local climates. Medieval Scandinavians also were artisans who worked with metal, wood, and leather, and while Viking merchants mostly traded fairly close to home, Scandinavian trade routes, in fact, extended as far south as the Middle East and as far east as the Dnieper River, with further connections to the ancient Silk Road via trading posts and cities to the east and south of Viking territories.

In the parts of Scandinavia that were warm and fertile enough for agriculture, farmers grew crops such as barley and rye, pulses, cabbage, and hops. In addition, hemp for ropemaking and flax to spin and weave into linen cloth were also important agricultural products.[i] Cows and goats were kept for their milk, and sheep for their wool and meat. Pigs were raised for their meat, and poultry for their feathers, down, and eggs.[ii] The diet provided by farm produce was supplemented by fishing, hunting, and gathering wild foods such as berries, nuts, and herbs.[iii]

Whether situated on a lonely farmstead or gathered into a village or town, the typical Viking dwelling was a longhouse with two or more sections. One end functioned as a byre for the domestic livestock, where their body heat helped to keep the house warm during the long, frigid Scandinavian winters. At the other end of the house was the space used for eating, sleeping, and tasks that often needed to be done indoors, such as spinning and weaving. Chieftains might have additional rooms, including one section that was used as the ceremonial hall in which they entertained guests and the warriors who fought for them.[iv] These great halls were also the places in which skalds recited their poetry in praise of the chieftain and where feasts in connection with religious sacrifices took place.[v]

Lowly farmhouses, the proud halls of the chieftains, and every sort of dwelling in between had a narrow firepit running down the length of the portions of the building used by the humans who lived there. The fire provided light, warmth, and heat to cook with, but it also created smoke that was not guided to the outside by a chimney; the sole escape for smoke was a small hole in the roof.[vi]

Towns, such as the important market center of Hedeby on the Jutland Peninsula, also might have workshops and warehouses in addition to dwellings. Further, archaeological evidence from Hedeby shows efforts at civil engineering in the form of wood-paved streets and wooden linings for the wells and the stream that ran through the town, presumably to keep the streets from churning into mud and to help keep the water supply as clean as possible.[vii] It's probably fair to say that Hedeby was not the only community to engage in projects like these, which were aimed at improving the quality of life for the residents, but one wonders whether that sort of effort was also made by communities outside the larger and more prosperous towns.

Families and Gender Roles

The basic Viking family unit was what we call the nuclear family: a husband, a wife, and their children. However, many families fit into a larger household unit, which could include servants or slaves or both in addition to the basic family unit. Households also occasionally encompassed two or more nuclear families—plus servants or slaves, if any—living together and working the same land.[viii]

Gender roles in Viking society were strongly circumscribed. Men dealt with the things outside the house, while women dealt with the things inside. In practical terms, this meant that women managed the household, cared for the children, and were responsible for tasks such as spinning and weaving, sewing clothing, baking bread, cooking or preserving food, and brewing beer. Women were also responsible for collecting milk and making cheese and butter.

Men worked the land and went hunting or fishing, and they were also involved in judicial proceedings and other governing work, which women were forbidden to undertake.[ix] In areas where agriculture was difficult or impossible because of climactic conditions, men's work shifted to animal husbandry, hunting of marine mammals and other animals, and fishing, or some combination thereof.[x] Men also were the ones who fought and went on raids, but those who had families and farms to tend usually stayed home; the fierce, plundering Vikings with which modern people are familiar usually were younger, unmarried males who had little or no land of their own and who joined raiding parties in an attempt to bolster fortunes that were unlikely to be improved through the inheritance of family wealth.[xi]

That said, there is some evidence for the adventuresome nature of Viking women, some of whom fought alongside men and others of whom embarked on dangerous journeys, either on their own behalf or with male relatives. Much of the evidence for the existence and deeds of these women is found in the Icelandic sagas, including the

Saga of Ragnar Lothbrok, in which one female warrior, Lagertha, plays an important role. A different version of Lagertha's story also appears alongside tales about other women warriors in the *Gesta Danorum* ("Deeds of the Danes"), a monumental history of Denmark written in the twelfth century by Danish historian Saxo Grammaticus.[xii]

While it is difficult to separate fact from fiction in the sagas and even in Saxo's carefully written history, physical evidence for Viking women as fighters is rather more reliable: an archeological study performed in 2017 confirmed that a Viking warrior who was buried at Birka in Sweden was indeed female.[xiii] In addition to the woman's skeleton, the authors of the paper report that the grave held "a sword, an axe, a spear, armour-piercing arrows, a battle knife, two shields, and two horses, one mare and one stallion; thus, the complete equipment of a professional warrior."[xiv] An examination of the skeleton's proportions and other attributes strongly suggested that the buried person was a woman, and later DNA testing confirmed female gender.[xv]

We don't know the name of the female warrior from Birka, but one adventurous woman in the saga literature who apparently was a real historical figure was Aud the Deep-Minded, the wife of the Viking king of Dublin, who lived in the ninth century. When Aud's husband was killed in battle, she packed up her entire household and moved everyone and everything to Iceland, where her brothers were already living.[xvi] Another historical figure is Freydis Eiriksdottir. Freydis was the sister of Leif Eiriksson (also commonly spelled as Erikson), the Viking who sailed to what is now Newfoundland in Canada in the eleventh century. The *Greenland Saga* tells the story of Freydis' organization of an expedition to Newfoundland on her own behalf sometime after her brother had constructed a small settlement there. This saga paints Freydis as a strong, ruthless, and conniving leader who is not above murdering those who stand in her way.[xvii]

Although some women did remain single and made their living by hiring themselves out for work, most women married.[xviii] Author

Kirsten Wolf points out that before the advent of Christianity, marriage in Viking society was primarily a business arrangement between the man and the woman, and marrying for love seems to have been unknown.[xix] Negotiations for marriage were carried out between the woman's father and her suitor or her suitor's family, and she had little to no choice in the matter. However, women were able to seek divorce of their own accord and had a right to take their dowry (money paid by the woman's father to her spouse's family upon marriage) and personal property with them when they left the marriage. The woman also had the right to get the bride price (money paid to her father by the groom's family) if it turned out her husband was at fault for the dissolution of the marriage.[xx] As Wolf notes, Christianity radically changed attitudes toward marriage and divorce by conceptualizing marriage as a sacrament between the spouses that was intended to last until one or both of the partners died rather than a business deal that could be dissolved at will should it become unsatisfactory to one or both of the partners.[xxi]

For men, women, and children alike, life in medieval Scandinavia was difficult and full of hard work. Only those with higher social status might expect to escape at least some of the physical labor that most members of society had to do in order to provide for themselves and their families. Rudimentary medical care, chronic malnutrition, and a complete lack of vaccinations of any kind meant that disease was both distressingly common and often fatal and that lifespans were relatively short.[xxii] To reach one's sixtieth birthday was to achieve an advanced age, according to Anders Winroth.[xxiii]

The evidence for Winroth's conclusions comes from the examination of skeletons from Viking-era graves. Adult height is dependent on nutrition in childhood and, as Winroth reports, Viking adults were often fairly short by modern Western standards. Examinations of Danish Viking skeletons shows that women on average were only slightly over five feet tall (158 centimeters on average) and men were only about six inches or so taller (171 centimeters on average). Further, many of the skeletons show evidence of disease, iron deficiency, and broken bones.[xxiv] However, author Neil Oliver presents a rosier picture, stating that the average male height was about five feet eight inches (about 173 centimeters) and the average female height about five feet three inches (about 160 centimeters) and that teeth examined from Viking burials "suggests many people enjoyed a reasonable diet."[xxv] That said, whether one accepts Winroth's or Oliver's data as more representative of the health of medieval Scandinavians, to be a Viking one had to be tough, not just in terms of warfare but in terms of mere survival in living conditions that many modern people would consider difficult at best and appalling at worst.

Longships

At the end of the eighth century, Scandinavians expanded their interactions with the outside world. Sometimes these interactions came in the form of Viking raids, but more often they came in the form of trade relationships or colonization of new lands. These expansions had far-reaching effects, so much so that author Anders Winroth observes that the "overall impact of Scandinavian endeavors was, unexpectedly, to stimulate the economy of Western Europe," which had collapsed in the wake of the fall of Rome and was still struggling to recover three hundred years later.[xxvi]

The piece of technology that gave the Vikings an advantage in these undertakings was the longship. Living as they did in areas with long coastlines and relatively short journeys to the sea from most inland locations, the ancient Scandinavians were quick to develop boatmaking technologies. Petroglyphs from the Bronze Age indicate that Scandinavians had already been seafaring peoples for over two thousand years before the Viking Age began.[xxvii]

The longships sailed by the Vikings were clinker-built, meaning that they were constructed of overlapping planks riveted together and then coated with a sealant, usually tar or oil made from seal blubber, to keep them from rotting.[xxviii] Viking shipwrights also caulked the places where the planks overlapped with animal hair in order to make the ships watertight.[xxix]

Today, we tend to have an image of Viking ships as having one square sail and many oars, but that was a later development; earlier ships had neither mast nor sail and were instead propelled by oars alone.[xxx] On inland journeys along rivers, the ships might also be unloaded, and both ship and cargo would be carried from one point to another along stretches of the river that were unnavigable.[xxxi]

Although the basic pattern of all Viking ships was the same, they could be adjusted in length and beam in order to serve their intended purpose and in order to be able to function in the waters where they would be used. Wider ships might be used for trade because they could carry more cargo, and lighter, narrower ships might be used on rivers. But whatever their purpose, for raiding, trading, or exploration, longships were the most important piece of Viking technology and were the tools that connected medieval Scandinavians to the rest of the world.

The Vikings Abroad

Vikings as Traders

Vikings of course traded with one another within their own territories, but Viking trade routes also ran throughout Western and Central Europe, extending into the Arab Caliphate on the Iberian Peninsula and in the Middle East, Byzantium, and eastward into what are now Ukraine, Belarus, and Russia. These trade routes ran along the coastlines of Europe; through the Mediterranean, Caspian, and Black Seas; and along navigable rivers such as the Rhine, the Seine, the Dnieper, and the Volga. The easternmost portions of these trade routes gave the Vikings access to goods from the Far East and Southeast Asia, which traveled along the ancient Silk Road.[xxxii]

Goods exported from Scandinavia included amber, timber, walrus ivory, and honey.[xxxiii] Iron ore taken from bogs was in high demand outside Viking lands, as were furs, schist to turn into whetstones, and soapstone, which was shaped into vessels for cooking and eating.[xxxiv] Vikings, in turn, imported silk, spices, and jewelry from the East, while wine, glass, pottery, and weapons came from Western and Central Europe.[xxxv] The slave trade also was quite active at this time, with slaves being both imported and exported by Viking traders.[xxxvi]

One of the imports most valued by Vikings was silver. This often came into Scandinavia in the form of Arab coins called dirhams. Hoard after hoard containing hundreds of dirhams has been excavated in places such as Germany and Sweden. These hoards are important not only because they show Western European peoples in active trade with Arab countries but also because the coins are dated and therefore can give us an idea of when this trade was active.[xxxvii] Author Richard Hall reports that coins from Viking hoards indicate that "the eastern trade had started by the 780s, increased in the 860s–880s and grew dramatically to a peak in the 940s–950s. Thereafter decline set in as the central Asian silver mines were depleted."[xxxviii] Of course the increase in numbers of coins also tracks with the increase in Viking trade outside of Scandinavia, as well as with the increase in Viking raids.

The Vikings did not use these or any other coins as currency, however. Both Arab coins and gold and silver Christian sacred objects raided from church treasuries were often melted down and the metal exchanged for goods or services by weight. We know that the Vikings did not see dirhams and other foreign coinage as currency but rather as a source of raw metal because Viking hoards often contain both fragmentary and complete coins.[xxxix]

The expansion of Viking trade routes did more than stimulate the economy, provide livelihoods for producers of goods, and give Scandinavians access to exotic luxury items. The growth in trade was also a stimulus for the growth of towns, which could function as manufacturing, collection, and distribution hubs much more efficiently than the small groupings of farmsteads that had been the most common type of community before the eighth century.[xl]

We have already discussed some of the characteristics of the town of Hedeby in Jutland, which was one of the more important centers of trade in medieval Scandinavia. Places like Hedeby were permanent settlements that, in addition to dwellings, had multiple jetties for docking boats and workshops and warehouses for creating and storing goods. In addition to such towns, there were also smaller market centers that might exist only at certain times of the year, where traders would gather to buy, sell, and exchange their goods.[xli]

Kaupang in Norway was one such center. Kaupang may originally have been a village, but it appears to have become simply a market center by about 850.[xlii] Richard Hall reports that bead-making was one of the crafts pursued in Kaupang, and he also states that materials for making casted items such as brooches and materials for making jewelry have been found there.[xliii] Kaupang also has been a rich source of evidence for the kinds of things that were being imported into Viking lands from other places. According to Hall, these included

> drinking glasses, pottery jugs and lava quernstones from the Frankish Rhineland, ... an Anglo-Saxon penny, ... Slavonic and Jutlandic pottery, and ... beads ... that may have come from places as widespread as Ireland, Ribe, Byzantium, the Black Sea/Caspian Sea region, and the Near and Middle East.[xliv]

While medieval Scandinavia certainly wasn't a cosmopolitan place, it wasn't isolated either. Vikings were busy collecting and making items to trade, and their trading practices connected them to places and peoples throughout Europe, Asia, and the Middle East. Just as with the practices of agriculture, hunting, and fishing, making crafts and trading were the occupations of a significant portion of the population, a much greater portion than was engaged in the raids that we so often associate with Viking culture.

Viking Raids

The first recorded Viking raid was on Portland in England in 789. The next reported raid, on the wealthy Northumbrian island monastery of Lindisfarne in 793, was even more violent than the one on Portland had been. Medieval English annals such as the *Anglo-Saxon Chronicle* record the terror and shock engendered by the Lindisfarne raid, wherein many of the monks were killed, others taken as slaves, and the monastery's treasury emptied of its gold, silver, silk vestments, and other valuables.[xlv] The sack of Lindisfarne was followed in 795 by another monastery raid, this time on Iona in the Inner Hebrides off the Scottish coast.[xlvi] With these three raids, the Viking Age is considered to have begun in earnest.

England was not the only target of Viking raids. The Frankish Empire also promised rich takings, and by the middle of the ninth century, Vikings had made several incursions into Frankish territory in addition to continuing their attacks on English soil. In 845, Vikings sailed down the Seine and attacked Paris. This raid was led by a man apparently named Ragnar, who may or may not have been the Lothbrok of the saga.[xlvii] (Ragnar's identity will be explored in more detail in a later chapter.) A further expansion of the territories considered ripe for plundering happened in 859, when Björn Ironsides, who likely was an actual historical personage and was said to be Ragnar's son, raided Spain. Björn then went on to raid Luni on Italy's Ligurian coast the following year.[xlviii]

Thirst for riches and a desire to prove oneself in battle were certainly part of the impetus for Viking men to take ship and sail across the sea to loot cities and towns, but this is only a very small part of the picture. Various cultural, social, and political factors also came into play, making ninth-century Scandinavia a launching pad primed for piratical attacks on other countries. One of these certainly was the Viking warrior culture, which greatly prized and rewarded courage and martial skill. However, it was the political structure in the earlier part of the Viking Age that brought these warriors together and created a framework in which they could prosper in their raiding activities.

Prior to the tenth century, the basic political unit in much of Scandinavia was the chiefdom, which could be passed from father to son, but succession to chieftainship in fact was much more fluid. Viking law and tradition allowed inheritance from both the mother's and the father's side, and as author John Haywood observes, "any man possessed of royal blood ... was eligible for kingship. Illegitimacy was no bar."[xlix]

Although a distinguished line of descent certainly was considered meritorious when putting oneself forward as a candidate for chieftainship, one's lineage was by no means the only consideration; many other factors contributed to whether a man might attain chieftainship, and these factors also determined whether and for how long he would be able to retain that position. The chieftain was accepted as a leader, but the hierarchical relationship stopped there. To the warriors at his command, the chieftain was first among equals, not superior to them. Anders Winroth states that Viking warriors "were not simple mercenaries fighting for pay; they were independent-minded and proud warriors who would fight alongside those they were bound to in honorable relations of friendship."[l]

To keep faith with his warriors, the chieftain was expected to be generous in the distribution of booty and other gifts, as well as in holding feasts and drinkings to which the warriors would be invited and at which the skalds, or poets, would perform songs and poems praising the exploits of the chieftain and his warriors.[li] As Winroth reports, gifts from the chieftain to his warriors were not simply payment for services rendered but rather the discharge of one side of a mutual obligation, the other side of which was the warrior's military service at the chieftain's command.[lii]

The size of Viking raiding parties no doubt varied depending on the number and size of ships and the number of armed men available. Neil Oliver estimates that one type of longship, the *drakkar* or "dragon ship," so named for the dragon heads carved into the raised prow and stern, might have been "as much as 120 feet [about 36.6 meters] long and able to carry perhaps 80 armed men at a time."[liii] Richard Hall describes a ship excavated at Hedeby as having been "built in c. 985 and was 30.9 m (101 feet) long ... and probably carried about 60 oarsmen."[liv] However, Anders Winroth estimates that smaller ships may have been more commonly used. Winroth describes one ship excavated in Denmark, called *Skuldelev 5*, which was "a little more than eighteen meters [59 feet] long and had space for thirteen pairs of oars."[lv]

Raiding parties might encompass only a handful of ships, but some Viking armies might muster one hundred or more vessels, depending on the objective of the raid. One attack, on Canterbury and the port of London in 851, purportedly was made by 350 ships.[lvi] We don't have any information on the numbers of men carried in these ships, but if we estimate that each ship carried 40 men, the sack of Canterbury would have been accomplished by about 14,000 men. If these ships were of the larger type described by Oliver, those numbers might have been double. Viking warriors were bold, ruthless, and had been trained from a young age to handle weapons, so it is no surprise that the sighting of Viking sails on the horizon or of longships rowing down the river struck terror into the hearts of the people who were unfortunate enough to have been the targets of Viking raids.

Exploration and Colonization

Raiding was only one reason why Vikings sailed to other lands. Vikings also made attempts at colonization, some successful, some not, and some of these attempts also encompassed exploration of new lands beyond the boundaries of medieval Scandinavia. Iceland was first settled by Vikings in the ninth century, while Scandinavian colonies along the Volkhov River—where the Vikings were known as "Rus"—flourished during the Viking Age. Schoolchildren today learn about the exploits of Leif Eiriksson, who attempted a settlement in what is now Newfoundland in Canada. A different Viking incursion, this time into England in 865, was made not with the aim of pillaging and then going home but rather of establishing a permanent Danish colony on English soil.

The Vikings who wished to colonize England were known as the "Great Army" or sometimes the "Great Heathen Army," which was led by men named Ivar, Halfdan, and Ubbe.[lvii] Ivar is usually thought to be Ragnar's son Ivar the Boneless, and Ubbe is named as one of Ragnar's sons in Saxo's *Gesta Danorum*. (The identities of Ragnar's progeny are discussed in more detail in a later chapter.) Neil Oliver states that this army of Vikings numbered about three thousand, and it was a continuous presence in Anglo-Saxon territories for about thirty years.[lviii]

In 878, after the Vikings had fought and pillaged their way through a large swath of English territory, King Alfred of England was finally able to defeat one segment of the Great Army and make a peace treaty with them. The treaty ceded to the Vikings an enormous amount of land that came to be known as the "Danelaw," since these lands were governed under Scandinavian law, not English. The Danelaw's boundaries extended northward from the Thames as far as the border with Northumbria and Strathclyde, and westward and eastward to take up a good portion of central and eastern England. One legacy of the Danelaw can be seen in many English place-names. The particles -*by*, -*thorp* (or -*thorpe*), and -*thwaite* that appear in names such as Whitby ("white homestead"), Scunthorpe ("outlying farmstead that belongs to Skuma"), and Bassenthwaite ("meadow that belongs to the Bastun family") are all of Norse origin.[lix]

While the Danelaw was created in order to stem the violence of an invading Viking army, the Scandinavian settlements that were founded along the Volkhov River appear to have been an outgrowth of Viking trade with the peoples in that region. Archaeological excavations at the settlements of Staraya Ladoga and Novgorod have yielded a great deal of information about these colonies, whose Viking inhabitants were known as "Rus," the word that gives Russia its name.

Staraya Ladoga appears to have been founded sometime in the eighth century, initially as a market center. Excavations there have found items such as a full set of blacksmith's tools, a great deal of glass beads, and dirham coins.[lx] The configuration of burials and burial sites also shows that the Scandinavian population lived side by side with the Slavs who were native to the area. Types of graves, methods of burial, and the creation of separate Scandinavian and Slavic burial grounds all attest to the ways these two peoples lived together over a thousand years ago.[lxi]

Novgorod is a somewhat later settlement than Staraya Ladoga, having been founded in the middle of the tenth century. Medieval Novgorod is also surprisingly well preserved; many of the buildings that made up this medieval town have been unearthed in relatively good condition and are comprised of a mixture of dwellings and workshops. Excavated goods include brooches, amulets, furniture, clothing, toy swords made of wood and, perhaps most importantly, letters that were written on birch bark, which demonstrate that this was a literate population.[lxii]

In Viking settlements along the Volkhov and in the Danelaw, the Scandinavian immigrant population gradually merged with the local ones. The settlement of Iceland was a completely different situation, however, since at the time of the original Scandinavian settlements, Iceland was entirely unpopulated.

Scandinavians began to settle Iceland in the late ninth century. A history of Iceland written in the second quarter of the twelfth century by Icelander Ari Thorgilsson places the start of colonization around 870. Examination of ice core samples taken from Iceland's glaciers appears to corroborate this date, although some controversy exists over the accuracy of the dating method used, which is based on chemical signatures from lava flows.[lxiii] Richard Hall estimates that by 1095, there may have been between 40,000 and 100,000 people living in Iceland, a number he bases on a census taken of people who had the right to attend the *Althing*, Iceland's national assembly, in that year. Hall reports that the 1095 census enumerated 4,560 "free land-owning farmers" as the basis for the estimated total population.[lxiv] Hall does not give the method used for his estimate, but one may assume that it is based on some sort of known proportion of landowners to those who were landless.

The Viking expeditions to what is now Canada did not have the good fortune that had attended many settlements elsewhere. The place that the Vikings dubbed "Vinland," for its supposed wealth of grapevines, was first visited by Vikings as the result of an accident. A man named Bjarni Hejolfsson was sailing from Iceland to Greenland in 986 when he was blown off course and came within sight of what is now Labrador. However, Bjarni did not land there; instead, he turned around and sailed safely to Iceland.[lxv]

Bjarni's tale of his adventure caught the ear of Leif Eiriksson, the son of Eirik the Red, who founded the ill-fated Viking colony in southern Greenland. Eiriksson bought Bjarni's ship, put together a crew, and sailed westward. Leif sailed along the coast of this new land until he found a suitable place for a camp, where he and his crew constructed shelters. Leif called his settlement *Leifsbuthir*.[lxvi]

Although there were several attempts by Leif's brothers and sister to anchor the colony and populate it, nothing ever came of those efforts. Extant sagas, which were penned centuries after the event, tell of difficulties with Indigenous peoples that the Viking settlers called *skraelings*. Eventually, the Vikings gave up on their settlement in this new land. It would be several hundred years before other white settlers went there in search of fishing grounds, timber, and other resources.

For a long time, many modern historians doubted the veracity of the Vinland story. However, Norwegian archaeologist Anne Stine Ingstad worked on excavations throughout most of the 1960s and unearthed undeniable evidence of a Viking presence in a place called L'Anse aux Meadows in Newfoundland. The settlement there is now assumed to be what remains of Leifsbuthir.[lxvii]

Whether operating as traders along rivers or overland, or as raiders pillaging along foreign coastlines, or as explorers seeking new lands, Vikings were a vital presence throughout a significant portion of Europe, Asia, and the Middle East. Medieval Scandinavians brought terror to the places they looted and commerce to the places where they traded. It is impossible to imagine the Middle Ages without Vikings, whose culture and history are a testament to the ways in which the world has always been connected, centuries before our current modes of near-instant communication.

Viking Verbal Arts

Icelandic Sagas and the Sources of the Saga of Ragnar Lothbrok

The word "saga" has entered the modern lexicon as a term that evokes images of great journeys, heroism, epic battles, fantasy, and often a sense of pastness, even if the story itself is not set in either a real or imagined past. However, this is a more modern definition. "Saga," an Icelandic word, originally meant simply "story," "history," or "myth," and it was first used in English as a generic term to describe Scandinavian prose writings in the eighteenth century. The definition with which we are familiar today is the result of expansions of meaning adopted over the nineteenth and twentieth centuries but which ultimately has its basis in the type of stories and characters contained in the Icelandic sagas.

The original corpus of Icelandic sagas began to be compiled in the twelfth century after writing was introduced by missionaries as a part of the Christianization of Scandinavia, whereas previously the sagas had been transmitted orally. Modern scholars have divided the sagas into various genres depending on the content of the stories. In his translation of the Lothbrok saga, author Ben Waggoner notes that these genres are rarely completely watertight: sagas of one type often contain elements that are characteristic of another.[lxviii]

There are three main types of saga: the sagas of Icelanders, which are more or less historical tales about the settlers who first populated

21

Iceland in the Middle Ages; the kings' sagas, which are historical and pseudo-historical stories about Scandinavian kings; and the *Fornaldarsögur*, a term that Waggoner translates as "sagas of old times" but are more commonly known as "legendary sagas." These legendary sagas encompass Germanic myths and heroic legends.[lxix] Waggoner notes that the *Saga of Ragnar Lodbrok* is one of those that defies generic classification since Lothbrok's story combines elements of both the kings' sagas and the legendary sagas.[lx] This is because Lothbrok is depicted as a king in a pseudo-historical tale that includes such fantasy elements as dragon-slaying and enchanted cows and also because part of Lothbrok's saga draws directly from one of the most important legendary sagas, the *Saga of the Volsungs*, which is discussed in greater detail below. (Appendix A contains a synopsis of the *Saga of the Volsungs*.)

A fourth important source for medieval Scandinavian myths and poetry is the pair of compilations known as the *Prose* (or *Younger*) *Edda* and the *Poetic* (or *Elder*) *Edda*, which were written down by Icelandic historian Snorri Sturluson in the early thirteenth century. The *Poetic Edda* is a collection of Norse myths in poetic form, while the *Prose Edda* is a manual for poetic composition. The *Prose Edda* was Sturluson's attempt to capture and describe the structure and intricacies of the ancient Norse poetry known as skaldic verse. Like the *Poetic Edda*, the *Prose Edda* also contains many Norse myths.

The *Saga of Ragnar Lothbrok* is preserved in multiple manuscript sources, some of which are more complete than others. Waggoner states that the most complete version of the saga is in a manuscript compiled around 1400, which now resides in the Royal Danish Library in Copenhagen and which presents the *Saga of Ragnar Lothbrok* as a direct continuation of the *Saga of the Volsungs*.[lxxi] Waggoner notes that another manuscript in the Royal Danish Library preserves a slightly different version of Ragnar's story, but unfortunately that manuscript is not complete.[lxxii]

Adjunct to Ragnar's saga proper is the *Tale of Ragnar's Sons*, detailing the deeds and adventures of Ragnar's progeny after their father's death at the hands of King Ella of Northumbria. The primary source for this portion of the story is the so-called *Hauksbók*, a manuscript compiled in the early fourteenth century by Icelander Haukr Erlendson. The *Tale of Ragnar's Sons*, which may have been written by Erlendson himself, is only one of many different items in this manuscript, which Waggoner notes also contains "Christian writings, historical works, and mathematical texts."[lxxiii]

The last main source for Ragnar's story is the *Krákumál*, a 29-stave anonymous poem written in the twelfth century, probably somewhere in the Scottish islands.[lxxiv] The *Krákumál*, or "Kraka's Lay," purports to be Ragnar's death-song, which Ragnar delivers while in a pit full of venomous snakes, where he dies at King Ella's command. The *Krákumál* is written in *háttlausa*, a type of skaldic meter that employs the alliteration common to Germanic and Scandinavian poetry of this period but avoids the internal rhyme of the more formal *dróttkvaett*, or "court meter," about which more is written below.[lxxv] Each stanza of the *Krákumál* begins with a refrain ("We hewed them with our swords") and then goes on to describe Ragnar's exploits in battles with various kings and nobles in various far-flung places, most of which are not mentioned either in the text of the saga proper or in the *Tale of Ragnar's Sons*.

Two other ancillary sources for Ragnar's story are a fragment of an Icelandic saga about Swedish and Danish kings and a sixteenth-century copy of part of the now-lost *Saga of the Scyldings* (*Skjöldungasaga*), a tale about the Danish Scylding dynasty. The Scyldings also appear in the Anglo-Saxon tale *Beowulf*; Beowulf's friend, Hrothgar, is a member of this dynasty. Waggoner states that the fragment of Ragnar's saga having to do with the kings tells the tale of Ragnar's forebears, while the *Saga of the Scyldings* contains material that also appears in the *Tale of Ragnar's Sons*.[lxxvi]

A final source is neither an Icelandic saga nor an Old Norse poem but rather a historical work in Latin, the *Gesta Danorum* ("Deeds of the Danes"), which was written by the medieval Danish historian Saxo Grammaticus (c. 1160–c. 1220). This monumental work, comprised of a series of nine books, is a history of Denmark from ancient times to the twelfth century. It contains a narrative of Ragnar's life and deeds although, as with the saga proper, it is difficult to untangle fact from fiction in Saxo's history.[lxxvii]

Some elements are shared between the saga and *Gesta Danorum*—such as the dragon-slaying episode and the source of the nickname "Lothbrok"—but there are significant variations between these two versions of the life and deeds of Ragnar Lothbrok.[lxxviii] Various details such as the names and number of Ragnar's sons are different in Saxo's account, and some aspects of the plot and action in the *Gesta* are not the same as in the saga proper. For example, Saxo relates battles between Ragnar and "Karl," (presumably Charles the Bald of France, who reigned from 843 to 877), as well as Ragnar's conquest of the Hellespont, neither of which appear in the saga itself.[lxxix]

Ragnar's saga therefore participates both in the fluidity of an oral tradition, in which pieces of a story might vary from transmission to transmission, and also in the very human impulse to ground a story, no matter how fantastic, in a world with qualities familiar to readers and listeners. It also reflects the urge to connect people with the past, whether real or imagined, in an effort to understand how things came to be the way they are.

Skaldic Poetry

Reputation and fame were vitally important to Vikings, and in particular to Viking chiefs and kings. In an age before the advent of writing, one way to broadcast one's deeds was to employ a skald, or court poet, to create songs detailing what one had accomplished.

Skaldic poetry originally was an oral art form, but after the advent of Christianity, it began to be preserved in writing. Extant skaldic poems often are attributed to particular poets and, to a certain extent, can be used as historical sources since they involve descriptions of contemporary events and praise of contemporary dignitaries.[lxxx] These characteristics distinguish skaldic poetry from that found in the Eddas. Eddic poetry, in contrast to skaldic, is usually anonymous and deals with deeds of past heroes or with mythological subjects.[lxxxi]

The most common form used for skaldic poetry is the *dróttkvaett*, or "court meter." This is a complex form with strict rules about line length, syllable stress, alliteration, and rhyme. Each stanza of a poem in court meter has eight lines, which are composed as four sets of *ab* pairs. Each line must have six syllables, three of which must be stressed and three of which must be unstressed. The last syllable of each line must be an unstressed syllable. The *a* line must have two alliterative syllables, and the following *b* line must use that same alliteration on one syllable. Every line also has to have internal rhymes.

In addition to formal poetic structures, skaldic poetry employed an additional layer of complexity in the form of kennings. A kenning is an oblique way of referring to a person or object and has two parts: the base word and the determinant. In her book on Viking life, author Kirsten Wolf presents the example of "surf horse" as a kenning for "ship," where "horse" is the base word naming the object, and "surf" is the determinant that qualifies the base word.[lxxxii] "Surf horse" is a relatively simple and straightforward kenning; often these were significantly more abstruse.

Kennings were used not only to make the poems more complex and therefore more interesting but also to help the skald stick to the rules for the meter by creating additional syllables with their attendant stresses, vowels for rhyming, and initial sounds for alliteration.[lxxxiii] They were also a means by which the skald could show their creativity and skill with words since they had to make up circumlocutions for otherwise ordinary words in addition to fitting everything within the restrictions imposed by the meter. Considering that this poetry originally was composed and transmitted without writing the poems down, it must have taken both a great deal of training and practice, as well as a prodigious memory, to be a skald.

Skaldic poetry has a role to play within the *Saga of Ragnar Lothbrok*. In a few places, Ragnar speaks using skaldic verse, as does Kraka/Aslaug, Ragnar's third wife. Each instance of verse is an example of heightened speech, where the situation calls for something other than mere dialogue. The first of these is when Ragnar kills the dragon that has been keeping the young noblewoman Thora captive. After the dragon is dead, Thora asks the name of her savior, and Ragnar replies with a verse that gives hints about his identity but does not reveal his name. Other skaldic exchanges take place during Ragnar's courtship of Kraka/Aslaug. When Kraka/Aslaug arrives at Ragnar's ships having met the conditions of the riddle Ragnar sets her, she announces her presence in verse. At the end of this first encounter, Ragnar uses skaldic verse to offer Kraka/Aslaug one of his first wife's shirts as a gift. Kraka/Aslaug declines the gift, which is also done in skaldic verse.

These poetic utterances serve two main purposes. One of these is a kind of solemnization of the moment, because the characters break out of normal speech patterns and use highly structured poetic language to convey what they want to say. The other is a revelation of social status: when Ragnar answers Thora's request for his name by using poetry and when Kraka/Aslaug uses poetry to address Ragnar later in the saga, both Ragnar and Kraka/Aslaug are indicating that they are of high social status because they are able to spontaneously construct and deliver skaldic verse, a form of poetry associated with noble and royal courts.

That Ragnar speaks in skaldic verse in the dragon-killing scene is important because it lets Thora know that despite his outlandish dress, her savior is her social equal and therefore it will be possible for Thora to marry him without shame. A similar condition is found in the exchanges between Kraka/Aslaug and Ragnar, where Ragnar's use of skaldic verse indicates his status as king and advertises his intelligence as a quality a woman might want in a husband. Kraka/Aslaug's use of verse also reveals something of her identity by showing that although she appears to be the daughter of peasants, she is in fact of much nobler stock and worthy to be Ragnar's wife and queen to his people. Thora, by contrast, does not need to speak in skaldic verse because her social position and lineage are never hidden and never in question. The same goes for Lagertha, Ragnar's first wife, who is a queen and warrior in her own right.

As we saw earlier, one of the sources for Ragnar's story is the *Krákumál*, or "Kraka's Lay." Evidently the snippets of poetry sprinkled into the saga proper were not enough for the person who composed the lay; they found it necessary to put into Ragnar's mouth an entire, extensive poem detailing his exploits, even going so far as to add adventures to which the saga does not testify. In one sense, then, the *Krákumál* might be seen as an early, poetic form of fan fiction.

Although it is ill-advised to take either skaldic poetry or the sagas at face value as historical sources, they nevertheless provide us with some nuggets of actual history. However, their true worth is not as witnesses to historical events but rather to the worldview of the people who created and compiled these stories. Through sagas and skaldic poetry, we learn which human qualities were most esteemed by the people that produced them, how cultural and social practices were seen and valued, and the skill and breadth of the imaginations of their creators.

Who Was Ragnar Lothbrok?

Like King Arthur and Robin Hood, Ragnar Lothbrok may have been a real person who may have done some of the deeds attributed to him in the sagas and related sources such as the *Krákumál*, and in medieval chronicles that record Viking activities. However, as with King Arthur and Robin Hood, it is not always easy to separate truth from fiction with respect to Ragnar Lothbrok. Dragon-slaying obviously falls onto the fictional side of things, but Viking raids in England, Norway, and France, and battles with Swedish kings are historically plausible, whether or not they actually happened as described in the saga.

One part of the problem is that sources purporting to be true histories were written down centuries after Lothbrok's supposed lifetime, and another part is the difficulty in figuring out whether the "Ragnar" named in a particular medieval chronicle is the "real" Ragnar Lothbrok (assuming such a person ever existed) or if it was someone else with the same name. Frankish chronicles mention one "Reginheri," who sacked Paris in 845, and a "Reginarius," who received land and a monastery from Charles the Bald in 840, while a Norse king named "Ragnall" is mentioned in Irish chronicles as having invaded Ireland in 851. Because of the paucity of sources and corroborating evidence, it is impossible to say whether any or all of these men were Ragnar Lothbrok. It is also possible that Reginheri, Reginarius, and Ragnall were all separate individuals and that none of them were Lothbrok.

The evidence for the existence of Lothbrok's sons is only slightly less shaky than that for Lothbrok himself. Björn Ironsides appears to have been an actual historical personage, and Sigurd Snake-in-the-Eye may have been as well, although whether they were really the sons of a historical Ragnar Lothbrok is an unanswered question. Ivar the Boneless and his brother Ubbe (mentioned in Saxo Grammaticus' *Gesta Danorum* but not in the saga) are credited by an addition made to one manuscript copy of the late ninth-century *Anglo-Saxon Chronicle* with having led a Viking army that invaded England in 878.[lxxxiv] According to author R. Bartlett, Abbo of Fleury, who wrote around 986, names Ivar and Ubbe as the killers of King Edmund (later St. Edmund the Martyr).[lxxxv] Ivar's and Ubbe's names also appear in a bevy of other later medieval histories of England, whose authors credit them with other depredations such as the destruction of Ely.[lxxxvi]

We may never know whether some of these people actually existed, nor may we ever know what their exact relationship, if any, to the putative Lothbrok may have been. However, we do know that lineage was of vital importance in medieval Scandinavian society and that to be able to claim descent from a famous personage or even from a divine being conferred status. At least one compiler of Ragnar's saga attempted to increase Ragnar's own status and thus the status of his sons through Ragnar's relationship by marriage to the Volsungs, one of the most important families in medieval Scandinavian myths and legends. This family's story is told in the *Saga of the Volsungs*, and it is a tale of dragons, cursed gold, love triangles, battles, and magic that inspired the medieval imagination and later was an important influence on more modern creators, such as opera composer Richard Wagner and author J. R. R. Tolkien.

The version of Ragnar's legend mentioned above treats it not as ancillary to the *Saga of the Volsungs* but rather a direct branching off from it. It takes up where the story of the Volsung Sigurd Fafnirsbane and his beloved Valkyrie Brynhild leaves off, with the escape of Heimer, Brynhild's foster-father, and the child Aslaug after the death of Sigurd and Brynhild, who are Aslaug's parents and two of the most important characters in the *Saga of the Volsungs*. Ragnar eventually takes Aslaug as his third wife, initially not knowing that she is the daughter of Sigurd and Brynhild, since when Ragnar meets her, she is living with peasants and goes by the name Kraka. It is not until much later in Ragnar's saga that Aslaug reveals her true lineage and proves it by saying that her next child will be a boy with a snake in his eye in honor of his maternal grandfather, who killed the dragon Fafnir. Aslaug's prophecy comes true, and the boy is named Sigurd Snake-in-the-Eye.

Not only was it important for Ragnar and his sons by Kraka/Aslaug (Björn, Ivar, Sigurd, and Hvitserk) to be able to claim the connection to the hero Sigurd and his lover Brynhild; it also allowed Ragnar and his children to claim a direct family relationship to Odin the All-Father himself. Volsung, the founder of the Volsung clan, was Kraka/Aslaug's grandfather, while Odin, in turn, was Volsung's great-grandfather. What greater legitimacy can one claim than to be descended from or married into the family of the most powerful god of the Norse pantheon?

Regardless of Ragnar's actual historicity, his character had an important influence on Scandinavian culture and society. Claiming someone like Ragnar Lothbrok as a forebear conveyed a certain amount of personal cachet and legitimacy that one might use to one's advantage. In the introduction to his translation of Ragnar's saga, author Ben Waggoner gives the example of Snorri Sturluson, the twelfth-century compiler of the Icelandic Eddas, who could claim descent from Björn Ironsides.[lxxxvii] Author Jackson Crawford, in his translation of the saga, states that Harald Fairhair (d. c. 930 CE), the first king of the united kingdom of Norway, claimed that Sigurd Snake-in-the-Eye was his grandfather.[lxxxviii]

These sorts of claims did not die with the Middle Ages: they were still being made in more modern times, also with the aim of establishing political and social legitimacy. In 1879, author Albert Welles published a genealogy of American President George Washington, claiming that Washington was a descendant of a man named Odin, whom Welles says assumed the name of that deity later in his life.[lxxxix] Welles' genealogy of course includes Ragnar Lothbrok and his sons among Washington's forebears via Thorfinn the Dane, who according to Welles migrated to England from Denmark in the early eleventh century and settled in Yorkshire, which was then part of the Danelaw.[xc] Of course the accuracy of Welles' genealogy is suspect, at least with regard to the generations before Thorfinn, because Welles uncritically assumes that everyone named in his sources must have been an actual historical person. Nevertheless, it is interesting to note that Ragnar and his progeny are still appearing in politically-motivated genealogies even one thousand years after their lifetimes.

In the end, however—and despite all attempts by others to increase their status by claiming Ragnar as an ancestor—it does not really matter whether the Lothbrok of the saga was an actual historical personage or a composite around whom a complex of legends, both historical and fictional, was woven, or whether he was made up out of whole cloth by an ancient storyteller. Ragnar's saga is a tale worth telling in and of itself, a tale about believable, sympathetic characters and a tale from which we can learn much about Viking culture and society.

[1]Notes to The World of Ragnar Lothbrok

Kirsten Wolf, *Daily Life of the Vikings* (Westport: The Greenwood Press, 2004), p. 22.

[1] Wolf, *Daily Life*, p. 22.

[1] Wolf, *Daily Life*, p. 22.

[1] Richard Hall, *The World of the Vikings* (New York: Thames and Hudson, 2007), pp. 40-43.

[1] Anders Winroth, *The Age of the Vikings* (Princeton: Princeton University Press, 2014), pp. 138-9.

[1] James Graham-Campbell, ed., *Cultural Atlas of the Viking World* (Oxford: Andromeda, 1994), p. 63.

[1] Graham-Campbell, *Cultural Atlas*, pp. 80-83.

[1] Wolf, *Daily Life*, p. 8.

[1] Wolf, *Daily Life*, pp. 10-11.

[1] Wolf, *Daily Life*, pp. 22-24.

[1] Winroth, *Age of the Vikings*, pp. 164-65.

[1] The stories of women warriors in Saxo's history are summarized in Judith Jesch, *Women in the Viking Age* (Woodbridge: The Boydell Press, 1991), pp. 176ff.

[1] Charlotte Hendenstierna-Jonson et al., "A Female Viking Warrior Confirmed by Genomics," *American Journal of Physical Anthropology* 164/4 (2017): 853-60.

[1] Hendenstierna-Jonson et al., "Female Viking Warrior," p. 855.

[1] Hendenstierna-Jonson et al., "Female Viking Warrior," p. 855-57.

[1] Hall, *World of the Vikings*, p. 34.

[1] Jesch, *Women in the Viking Age*, pp. 183-85.

[1] Wolf, *Daily Life*, p. 13.

[1] Wolf, *Daily Life*, pp. 8-9.

[1] Wolf, *Daily Life*, p. 10.

[1] Wolf, *Daily Life*, p. 10.

[1] Winroth, *Age of the Vikings*, pp. 162-64.

[1] Winroth, *Age of the Vikings*, pp. 162-64.

[1] Winroth, *Age of the Vikings*, pp. 163-64.

[1] Neil Oliver, *The Vikings: A New History* (New York: Pegasus Books LLC, 2013), p. 108.

[1] Winroth, *Age of the Vikings*, p. 123.

[1] John Haywood, *Northmen: The Viking Saga AD 793-1241* (New York: St. Martin's Press, 2015), p. 14.

[1] Wolf, *Daily Life*, p. 24; Graham-Campbell, *Cultural Atlas*, p. 75.

[1] Haywood, *Northmen*, pp. 20-22; Graham-Campell, *Cultural Atlas*, p. 75.

[1] Haywood, *Northmen*, p. 22.

[1] Graham-Campbell, *Cultural Atlas*, p. 75.

[1] Graham-Campbell, *Cultural Atlas*, p. 79.

[1] Wolf, *Daily Life*, p. 24.

[1] Graham-Campbell, *Cultural Atlas*, p. 78.

[1] Graham-Campbell, *Cultural Atlas*, p. 78.

[1] Hall, *World of the Vikings*, pp. 33, 99.

[1] Hall, *World of the Vikings*, p. 101.

[1] Hall, *World of the Vikings*, p. 101.

[1] Winroth, *Age of the Vikings*, pp. 124–27,

[1] Graham-Campbell, *Cultural Atlas*, p. 78.

[1] Graham-Campbell, *Cultural Atlas*, p. 85.

[1] Hall, *World of the Vikings*, p. 59.

[1] Hall, *World of the Vikings*, p. 60.

[1] Hall, *World of the Vikings*, p. 60. Ribe is a town in Denmark.

[1] Haywood, *Northmen*, pp. 42–3.

[1] Haywood, *Northmen*, p. 45.

[1] Haywood, *Northmen*, pp. 45, 88.

[1] Haywood, *Northmen*, pp. 169–70.

[1] Haywood, *Northmen*, p. 40.

[1] Winroth, *Age of the Vikings*, p. 136.

[1] Winroth, *Age of the Vikings*, pp. 136–39.

[1] Winroth, *Age of the Vikings*, pp. 136–37.

[1] Oliver, *New History*, pp. 99–100.

[1] Hall, *Vikings*, p. 54.

[1] Winroth, *Age of the Vikings*, p. 75.

[1] Haywood, *Northmen*, p. 47.

[1] Haywood, *Northmen*, p. 50.

[1] Oliver, New History, p. 169.

[1] Caroline Taggart, *The Book of English Place Names: How Our Towns and Villages Got Their Names* (n. p.: Ebury Press, 2011), pp. 15, 82, 269.

[1] Graham-Campbell, *Cultural Atlas*, pp. 190-91; Winroth, *Age of the Vikings*, p. 114.

[1] Graham-Campbell, *Cultural Atlas*, pp. 190-91.

[1] Graham-Campbell, *Cultural Atlas*, p. 192; Hall, *Vikings*, p. 97.

[1] Hall, *Vikings*, pp. 150, 152.

[1] Hall, *Vikings*, p. 151.

[1] Hall, *Vikings*, p. 181.

[1] Hall, *Vikings*, p. 160.

[1] Hall, *Vikings*, p. 161.

[1] Ben Waggoner, trans., *The Sagas of Ragnar Lodbrok* (New Haven: The Troth, 2009), p. xiii.

[1] Waggoner, *Sagas of Ragnar Lodbrok*, p. xi.

[1] Waggoner, *Sagas of Ragnar Lodbrok*, p. xiii.

[1] Waggoner, *Sagas of Ragnar Lodbrok*, p. xxiv. The manuscript in question is Copenhagen, Royal Danish Library, MS NkS 1824b 4to.

[1] This manuscript is Copenhagen, Royal Danish Library, MS AM 147 4to. Waggoner, *Sagas of Ragnar Lodbrok*, p. xxiv.

[1] Waggoner, *Sagas of Ragnar Lodbrok*, p. xxv. Waggoner also notes that the *Hauksbók* was broken up into its constituent pieces, and the pieces were rebound and catalogued separately. The portion containing the *Tale of Ragnar's Sons* now resides in the Arnamagnaean Institute at the University of Copenhagan as MS AM 544.

[1] Robert Crawford, *Scotland's Books: A History of Scottish Literature* (Oxford: Oxford University Press, 2009), n. p., accessed through Google Books <http://google.com/books> 23 March 2020.

[1] n. a., "Teutonic Forms," p. 3 (PDF accessed via https://www.jsicmail.ac.uk, 23 March 2020). The PDF appears to cite Turville-Petre, p. xix, as a source for the definition of *háttlausa* but does not give a bibliographical description beyond the author's surname and page number. It is possible that this information was taken from *Scaldic Poetry* by Gabriel Turville-Petre (Oxford: Clarendon Press, 1976), p. xxix, but I do not have access to this volume and so cannot confirm the accuracy of this assumption.

[1] Waggoner, *Sagas of Ragnar Lodbrok*, p. x.

[1] Oliver Elton, trans. *The Nine Books of the Danish History of Saxo Grammaticus*. 2 vols. (London: Norroena Society, [1905]).

[1] Elton, trans., *Saxo Grammaticus*, vol. 2, pp. 544–5.

[1] Elton, trans., *Saxo Grammaticus*, vol. 2, pp. 550 (Charlemagne episode) and 552–4 (Hellespont episode).

[1] Winroth, *Age of the Vikings*, pp. 134–38.

[1] Wolf, *Daily Life*, p. 55.

[1] Wolf, *Daily Life*, p. 55.

[1] Crawford, *Volsungs,* p. xv.

[1] R. Bartlett, "The Viking Hiatus in the Cult of Saints as Seen in the Twelfth Century," in *The Long Twelfth-Century View of the Anglo-Saxon Past*, edited by Martin Brett and David A. Woodman (Abingdon: Routledge, 2016), p. 18. Bartlett cites the F manuscript of the *Chronicle*, f. 54. "Viking Hiatus," n. 16.

[1] Bartlett, "Viking Hiatus," pp. 17–8.

[1] Bartlett, "Viking Hiatus," p. 18.

[1] Waggoner, *Sagas of Ragnar Lodbrok*, pp. xvi–xvii.

[1] Crawford, *Volsungs,* p. xix.

[1] Albert Welles, *The Pedigree and History of the Washington Family* (New York: Society Library, 1879).

[1] Welles, *Washington*, p. iv.

Part II: The Saga of Ragnar Lothbrok and His Sons

The version of the saga presented here is a compilation taken from various modern translations and retellings of the story of Ragnar's life and deeds and those of his sons. I have not made any attempt to indicate which parts of the story told here come from which portion of the medieval sources; rather, my goal has been to create a coherent narrative that is accessible to modern readers.

The portions of the saga's dialogue that exist as skaldic poetry have been freely rewritten based on modern translations of the Old Norse. I have used both alliteration and kennings in the poetic sections in an attempt to capture something of the flavor of the original Old Norse poetry, but I have not employed actual skaldic poetic form. The kennings for "dragon" in the poem recited by Ragnar are original to the Old Norse, but the kenning for "black" in the poem recited by Kraka/Aslaug is my own addition.

From time to time, the saga presents ideas or images that deserve further explanation. In order to provide greater context for the modern reader, I have appended notes for these items at the foot of the saga.

Ragnar Becomes King

Once there was a king named Sigurd Ring. He had a fair wife named Afhild, and together they had a son named Ragnar. Ragnar grew into a handsome young man, strong and well made in his body.

When Ragnar was fifteen years old, his mother died. After a suitable period of mourning, Sigurd began to look for a new wife. He set his heart upon Alfsol, the daughter of the king of Jutland. Sigurd sent messengers to Jutland, asking for Alfsol's hand. When Alfsol's father heard the message, he scoffed. He said to the messenger, "Take this answer back to your master. Say to him, 'Sigurd Ring may be a great king, but he is an old man. My daughter is worthy of a better husband than one who is likely to die if not on his wedding night then certainly soon thereafter.'"

When Sigurd heard the king of Jutland's reply, he flew into a rage. "An old man am I, with one foot in the grave? The churl who sits upon the throne of Jutland will regret his reply to me. I will make him eat those words at the point of my spear and take his daughter to wife whether he wills it or no."

Sigurd assembled his army and marched upon Jutland. The Jutlanders fought well and valiantly, but they were no match for Sigurd's men. Soon it became clear that Sigurd would be the victor, and rather than allowing him to take Alfsol by force, her father gave her a goblet of poison to drink, and so she died.

After the battle, Alfsol's body was found by Sigurd's men. They carried it carefully back to their king, who began to weep and mourn when he saw that the fair young woman was dead and that she had died by poisoning.

"Fetch my best ship, and build upon it a pyre," said Sigurd. "I will give Alfsol a good funeral, one fit for a queen, even though she did not live to become one."

The ship was pulled up onto the shore, and Alfsol's body was laid upon a pyre as though she had been a queen. Sigurd stood next to the ship as the pyre was kindled. When the mooring line was cut and the ship began to drift out with the tide, Sigurd sprang aboard and stood in the prow.

"If Alfsol could not join me as my wife in this life, I shall join her in death!" cried Sigurd as he drew his sword. "My son Ragnar is a brave and worthy man. Take him now to be your king!" Then Sigurd took the sword and plunged it into his breast. He fell into the flames, and so his body was burned along with Alfsol's.

And so it was that Ragnar became king, even though he was only fifteen years old. The men of his realm quickly learned to respect him, for his judgement was sound and none could match him in battle. Ragnar led his men on many raids and into many battles, and always they came back victorious, with the holds of their ships full of plunder. Ragnar himself escaped every fight without even a scratch, for his mother had woven him a magic shirt that kept him from all harm.

One of Ragnar's many raiding expeditions took him to Norway. When the battles and the raids were done, he and his men found a sheltered spot at which to beach their ships. They were weary and wanted to rest before sailing for home. They made camp and then spent the night on the beach.

In the morning, Ragnar desired to be alone. He took with him his sword and walked through the forest and up one of the many hills that surrounded the beach. The sky was clear, and the sun was bright, and Ragnar delighted in the beauty of the day.

When he reached the crown of one of the hills, Ragnar decided to sit upon the grass and enjoy the peaceful morning. As he looked out over the land, he saw two armies marching toward one another. The armies met and clashed, and soon it began to go very poorly indeed for one side. Ragnar watched more closely and perceived that the losing army was led not by a man but by a woman who showed such skill with her weapons that none could stand against her. Nevertheless, she could not conquer an entire army by her strength alone, and as her warriors fell one by one under the blades of her enemies, she found herself nearly surrounded and hard-pressed.

Ragnar drew his sword and ran to her aid. He fought so fiercely and with such strength that soon he and the woman between them put the other army to flight. Once the battle was over, the woman went to Ragnar and said, "I thank you for your aid. But for you, surely I would also lie dead on the field alongside so many doughty men. My name is Lagertha, and I rule the lands here. May I know your name that I may thank you properly?"

"I am Ragnar, son of Sigurd Ring, and a king among my own people," said Ragnar. "My men and I beached our ships near here. You are most welcome for my help. Never have I seen a shieldmaiden fight with such strength and skill."

"Come back to my stronghold with me," said Lagertha, "and bring your men with you. You will all be my guests at my victory feast."

That night, Ragnar and his men drank and feasted with Lagertha. By the end of the night, Ragnar had fallen in love with Lagertha, who he found to be wise and well-respected by her people. Ragnar proposed marriage, and Lagertha accepted on condition that they remain in her realm. "I would not be an idle consort, content merely to wait upon her royal husband. Here I rule, and here I shall stay."

Ragnar agreed to Lagertha's terms, and they spent three happy years together as husband and wife. At the end of the third year, Ragnar found himself becoming restless. He longed for voyages across the sea and adventures that led to battle and plunder in faraway places.

One day, a messenger came to Ragnar with news that his kingdom was endangered. Ragnar called for his armor and weapons, and caused a ship to be made ready. Then he went to Lagertha and said, "I must return to my own country. I have been away for too long, and now my kingdom is likely to fall. Come with me! Your skill in battle is unmatched, and I would be grateful for your help."

"When we wed, I told you that it was on condition that you remained here," said Lagertha. "I will not leave the throne of my land to become a retainer in yours. You must choose. Either you stay here as my consort, or we part ways forever."

"Then part we must," said Ragnar, "for I cannot forsake my own people. Farewell, and may good fortune smile upon you."

And so it was that Ragnar and Lagertha parted ways, never to see one another again in this world.

Ragnar and the Dragon

Once there was an Earl of Gautland named Herrud, who had a beautiful daughter named Thora. Herrud doted on his daughter. He gave Thora her own house to live in, and a day rarely passed without the earl giving Thora some present or other. One day, Herrud brought his daughter what looked like a small garden snake, which had been given to him by a merchant from a far-off land. The young woman delighted in the creature and made quite a pet of it. But unbeknownst to Thora and her father, the serpent was not a common snake: it was a baby dragon. The serpent continued to grow and grow until finally it was so large it could no longer fit inside Thora's house. It wrapped itself around the house, and because of its great love for Thora, it would allow no one to cross the threshold except the man who fed it a whole ox every day and who brought food and drink and other needful things to the young woman.

"This cannot stand," said the earl. "My daughter is a prisoner in her own home, and there is no warrior among my own people who is able to kill that dread beast. Send messengers throughout all the lands. Tell them that whoever slays that dragon may have my daughter's hand in marriage and a great deal of gold besides."

The messengers were duly sent, and soon one of them arrived at Ragnar's court. The messenger was given an audience with Ragnar, where he explained his errand to the young king.

"I come from the Earl of Gautland," said the messenger. "He seeks a champion to slay the dragon that keeps his daughter prisoner in her own home. The dragon is large and fearsome. Its fangs drip venom, and its very blood will poison anything it touches. There is no one in all of Gautland who has proven himself brave enough to face the beast, so the earl promises the hand of his daughter in marriage, and much gold besides, to whoever can slay the monster and come out of the battle alive."

"Tell me more of the earl's daughter," said Ragnar. "What manner of woman is she?"

"She is the fairest creature upon this earth," said the messenger. "I saw her once with my own eyes through a window of her house. She is comely of face and body, and her hair is golden and soft as silk. Any man would be proud to call her his wife, and doubtless many champions would have already fought to the death for the honor of her hand but for the interference of the dragon."

Ragnar thanked the messenger and ordered that he be given food and drink and a place to rest before going on his way. Then Ragnar began to think of how he might win Thora's hand for himself. He was very young, but he was king, and he knew that every king was in need of a queen. Surely there was no more worthy queen in the world than the daughter of Earl Herrud. Also, Ragnar had an adventurous spirit, and nothing tempted him quite so much as the chance to test his mettle against a fully grown dragon with venomous fangs and poisonous blood. But how to kill the beast without being poisoned himself?

Finally, Ragnar hit upon the solution. He called for breeches and a cloak to be made out of a shaggy goat's hide. When the garments were complete, Ragnar soaked them in pitch. As soon as the pitch had dried, Ragnar sailed for Gautland, bringing his best spear with him. Beaching his ship in a sheltered place that no one was likely to visit, he went ashore secretly, and dressed in his odd, shaggy clothing, he crept silently to Thora's house, where the dragon lay sleeping with its great coils wrapped around the walls.

Before the dragon could rouse itself to fight, Ragnar thrust at it with his spear and then drew the spear out again. The dragon screamed and went to attack, but Ragnar was too quick. Ragnar thrust again with his spear, and this time the point struck bone. Ragnar pulled the shaft of the spear out, but the shaft broke, and the head remained lodged in the dragon's body. As the dragon thrashed and screamed in its death throes, some of its blood splashed upon Ragnar, but he took no hurt because he was well protected by his odd, shaggy clothing. From that day forward, he was known as "Lothbrok," which means "shaggy breeches."

Thora looked out her window just as Ragnar was walking away. She saw that the dragon had been slain, and she rightly guessed that the man outside was the one who had killed it. Thora went out of her house and called to Ragnar. "Are you the one who slew the dragon? Please accept my thanks," she said.

Ragnar turned, and as he did so, Thora noted how very tall and broad he was, and how very strong and handsome.

"Yes, it was I who slew the beast," said Ragnar.

"Who are you?" asked Thora. "Tell me your name."

Ragnar spoke this verse in reply:

Your champion am I, beautiful lady,

Eighteen winters have I walked the earth.[xci]

Though young I am valiant, and vowed

To bring low the land-fish,[xcii]

Dread beast who besets you

With strength and spear

I vanquished the vile worm

Thrusting home to the very heart

Of the heath-salmon.[xciii]

Then Ragnar turned and walked away.

In the morning, Thora told her father that the dragon had been slain, and she took the earl to see its body. The Earl saw the end of the spear shaft sticking out of the beast's hide. He commanded that the end of the spear be removed. It took three strong men to pull it out, and when they finally had it in their hands, the three of them could barely lift it, even when they all tried together. The Earl marveled at this and asked Thora, "Who is this man? Surely he must be a great champion to wield such a mighty weapon. He deserves our thanks, and I have promised him your hand in marriage."

"I don't know who he is, Father," said the young woman. "I asked him his name, but he answered with a riddle and then walked away without saying anything else. All I know about him is that he is eighteen winters old, that he was very oddly dressed, and that he slew the dragon."

The Earl then decided that a great meeting should be held at his court to find out who his daughter's deliverer was. He sent messengers throughout all the lands, telling the champions to assemble and say whether it was they who had slain the dragon or not, and to bring proof that they had done the deed themselves, and not some other.

On the day of the meeting, Ragnar came into the earl's court along with the men of his ship. He brought with him the broken spear shaft, but he did not wear his shaggy clothing, for he did not want the earl's daughter to see him and identify him thereby.

When all the men had assembled in the hall, the earl thanked them for coming and explained what needed to be done. "The dragon that beset my household has been slain by a mighty spear. The head and part of the shaft were left behind in the beast's body. I will bring the head to each of you so that you may say whether it is yours or not. If you claim it, be prepared to prove it by producing the shaft of the spear. Whoever it is that did this deed will have my daughter's hand in marriage and much gold besides, as I have promised."

Then the earl caused the spearhead to be shown to each man in turn. Every one of them denied that it was theirs, even though they longed to say that it was and thus have the earl's daughter in marriage, for she was very beautiful indeed.

Finally, the spearhead was shown to Ragnar. "It is mine," he said. "With that spear, I slew the dragon."

"Prove it," said the earl, "and if you lie, know that it will go ill for you."

Ragnar produced the broken spear shaft, and the other piece was fitted to it. It was obvious that this was the man who had killed the dragon. The Earl proclaimed a great feast to celebrate the death of the beast, the courage and strength of Ragnar, and the marriage of his daughter to such a fine champion. At the feast, Ragnar took Thora to be his wife, and when the feasting was over, he took her to his own country, where they lived happily together for many years. Thora gave Ragnar two sons named Erik and Agnar. They grew into fine young men, both tall, handsome, and strong. None could best them, either in battle or in contests of sport.

A day came when Thora fell gravely ill. In a few days, she was dead. Ragnar mourned her greatly, and his sorrow was so deep that he could not abide to stay in the country where his beloved wife had died. Ragnar turned the rule of his kingdom over to his sons and advisers and then took ship to begin a life of adventure and raiding once again.

Aslaug

The mighty champion Sigurd, who slew the dragon Fafnir, had a daughter named Aslaug by the Valkyrie named Brynhild. At Sigurd's court, there was an exiled king named Heimer, who had been married to Brynhild's sister. Heimer was a gifted poet and harper, and so had been made Sigurd's skald. Heimer was Aslaug's foster-father, as he had been to her mother before her, and he doted on little Aslaug from the time she was a tiny infant.

When Aslaug was three years old, her parents died. Aslaug's father was murdered at the court of King Gjuki, where he then dwelled, and her mother died by her own hand in grief over Sigurd's death. Knowing that Aslaug was in danger from Sigurd's enemies, Heimer ran away with her. He made a large harp and concealed the child within it so that they might wander from place to place without anyone asking questions, since a skald traveling with his harp was nothing to be curious about.

After a long journey, Heimer and Aslaug arrived in Norway at a place called Spangarheith, where there was a lonely farmstead. The people of the farm were an old man named Aki and his wife, an old woman named Grima. Heimer went to the farmhouse and knocked on the door. When Grima answered, she said, "What is it you want? If you are looking for my husband, he is not here, but he will be back soon."

"I look for nothing but a fire to warm myself by and a place to sleep for the night," said Heimer, "and if you could also spare a crust of bread for a wandering skald, I will be most thankful."

"A fire is already kindled on my hearth, and you may sleep in our barn if you like," said the woman. "I have some bread that I baked yesterday that you are welcome to eat."

Heimer thanked the woman and went to sit by the hearth. He set down his harp and began to warm himself while the woman went back to her own work.

Now, when Heimer left Sigurd's court with little Aslaug, he also packed into the harp a quantity of gold and some of the girl's fine dresses, for she would need both when they finally reached a place of safety. Himself he had dressed in poor clothing, as befits a wandering skald, but he had forgotten to take off the lordly ring he wore upon one finger. The old woman caught a glint of gold when Heimer stretched out his hands to the fire, and when she examined his harp more closely, she saw a bit of fine cloth peeking out from the seam of the door that enclosed Aslaug and her belongings. This set the old woman to thinking about how she might relieve the stranger of his gold and fine cloth, but she said nothing to Heimer of what she had seen.

Presently, the old woman showed Heimer to the place where he was to sleep that night and then returned to her house. Not long after that, her husband came home and was angered to find that his dinner had not yet been prepared, for Grima had been dealing with their visitor instead of cooking a meal.

"Do not be vexed, husband," said Grima. "I saw a thing today that will surely bring us the fortune we have lacked. A wandering skald came to the door today, asking for warmth and shelter. I let him sit by the fire. But this is no ordinary skald. He has fine clothing packed away in that harp of his, and he wears a gold ring upon his finger."

"Yes?" said Aki. "What is that to us?"

"Old fool, don't you see?" replied Grima. "This is our chance! If we kill the skald, we can take his gold and his fine raiment and maybe even sell the harp. We'll never want for anything ever again!"

"This is a wicked thing you're planning, Grima," said Aki. "The skald is a guest in our house. It is a truly shameful thing to murder a guest and then rob him. I won't do it."

"Very well," replied the old woman. "Don't help me then. I'll just put you out to pasture, like a broken-down old horse, and take the skald for my husband. Or we could just kill you. The result will be the same in any case. I mean to live well and comfortably, even if you don't."

After a long quarrel, the old woman finally convinced her husband to help her kill Heimer and steal all of his possessions. Aki took up his axe, and then he and Grima crept silently into the barn where Heimer lay fast asleep with his harp by his side. Aslaug remained hidden within, for Heimer was not sure of her safety even among these poor people.

Grima picked up the harp and brought it back to the cottage, while Aki took his axe and struck Heimer a great blow on his head, killing him instantly. Then Aki went back to the cottage, where he found his wife attempting to open the harp. She was having great difficulty, for Heimer had had the harp constructed with a secret catch, and only he knew how to open it. Finally Grima became so frustrated that she took Aki's axe and broke the harp open. Imagine the surprise of the old couple when they found not just gold and fine raiment but also a beautiful young girl with golden hair concealed within!

"Well, this is a fine turn of events," said Aki. "What are we to do now? Are you thinking we should kill the child, too? I'll have you know that I will not harm a hair on her head, no matter how much you plead."

"No, we'll not kill her," said Grima. "We'll keep her. We could use another pair of hands around the farm. We'll just say she's our daughter."

Aki laughed aloud at this. "Have you looked at yourself, woman? Have you looked at me? We are both old and gnarled and ugly, and this child is the fairest I have ever seen. Surely her parents were both noble people. Who will ever believe us?"

"That's of no matter. We'll disguise her. Dress her in rags, cut her hair, smear her with ashes and mud, and she'll look enough like a peasant's child to pass for our own. And it's not like we have many visitors out here." Then Grima turned to the child and said, "What is your name, child?" but Aslaug was too frightened to reply. The old couple terrified her, and she wondered where her beloved Heimer had gone.

And so it was that Aki and Grima adopted Aslaug and raised her as their own. Since Aslaug could not or would not tell the old couple her name, the woman decided to call her Kraka, which means "crow," in honor of her mother, who also bore that name. Aslaug remained with Grima and Aki, and she grew into a lovely young woman. She retained her habit of silence and rarely spoke, even to her foster-parents. Even so, she was clever and canny, and her beauty was matched well by her wits. Aslaug lived with the old couple and worked for them like a slave, for she had no other choice, but never did she forget her parentage, nor did she ever forget how her beloved foster-father had met his death.

Ragnar and Aslaug

Aslaug, who was now called Kraka, was sixteen years old when Ragnar Lothbrok returned to the sea with his companions. They raided far and near, and after one such raid, they beached their ships near Spangarheith, where dwelt Grima and Aki and their foster-daughter. Ragnar told his cooks to take a measure of flour and other things needed to bake bread and to go find a willing cottager or baker who would help them. The cooks did as Ragnar asked, and once everything was assembled, they went looking for someone to help them bake the bread. Soon enough, they came across Grima and Aki's farmstead. They knocked on the door, and Grima answered.

"What is it you want?" she said.

"We are the companions of Ragnar Lothbrok," they replied. "We beached our ships not far from here. We have come to ask for help in baking bread. Now we have told you who we are. What is your name?"

"I am called Grima, and I would gladly help you, but my hands are too gnarled and stiff to knead bread anymore. I will call my daughter, and she will help you."

Now, Kraka had been out in the field tending to the cattle when she spied Ragnar's ships pulled up on the shingle of the beach. Thinking that some of the men might come to the farmstead, she went and bathed herself and washed her hair, things that Grima had forbidden her to do lest any man come across her and see how very beautiful she was.

Kraka entered the cottage just as the men were beginning to light a fire to bake the bread. When they saw the girl, they could not believe their eyes. They had never seen a woman so beautiful in all their travels.

"Is this young woman your daughter?" asked the men.

"Yes, indeed she is," said Grima.

"How can that be possible? She is the fairest of all women, and you are gnarled and hideous."

"Time has been unkind to me," said Grima. "You should have seen me in my younger days."

Grima told Kraka to help make the bread. Kraka complied, silently. She helped make the dough and knead it. When it was finally set to bake, the men were so entranced by Kraka that they lost track of time, and the bread was burned.

The cooks returned to their ships with the burned bread. When the meal was served later, all the men complained at how burnt the bread was. Ragnar said, "What happened? You are skilled cooks. You have never burnt the bread like this before."

"No, we have never burnt the bread like this before," said the senior cook, "but we had never seen a girl that beautiful before, either."

"Explain this," said Ragnar.

"Well," said the junior cook, "we found a farmstead and asked for help baking bread, as you asked us to do, and the old woman who lived there had her daughter help us. I swear to you I have never seen a lovelier woman in all my days. She was so entrancing that we kept our gaze fixed on her, and in so doing, we burned the bread."

Ragnar scoffed. "No woman has ever been that beautiful. Come now, tell us what really happened."

But the cooks would not change their tale. Finally Ragnar said, "Very well, if she is as lovely as you have said, go back to the farmstead and ask her to come and visit me here, for it is high time I took a wife again. But you must give her this message: say to her, 'Come to meet Ragnar Lothbrok, our king and the captain of the ships, but he commands that you must come neither dressed nor undressed, neither sated nor hungry, nor must you come alone, but no man may come along with you.'"

The cooks went back to the farmstead, where they found Grima and Kraka working together inside the cottage. They told Kraka what Ragnar said she should do. When Grima heard Ragnar's message, she scoffed. "What is he playing at, giving my daughter those ridiculous instructions? I think this king and captain of yours, if he really is both those things, might not be quite all there."

"No, I think there is a sound purpose behind this message, if only we can puzzle it out," said Kraka. Then she said to the cooks, "Thank your king and captain for his invitation. Tell him that I cannot come with you right now but that I will visit him in the morning."

The cooks went back to the ships and gave Ragnar Kraka's answer. During the night, Kraka thought hard about Ragnar's message and how she might do as he had bid. Finally she arrived at a solution and went to sleep.

In the morning, Kraka went to Aki and said, "I would like to borrow your trout net, please."

Aki thought this an odd request, but he gave her the net anyway. Kraka went to her chamber and took off all her clothes. Then she wrapped the net around herself as though it were a dress. When that was done, she went into the kitchen and took a bite of a leek that lay on the table. "Now I am neither dressed nor undressed, and I am neither sated nor hungry." Kraka turned to Aki once again. "Lend me your old dog so that I may not go alone, but with no man accompanying me."

Kraka went to the ships, the old dog trotting by her side. When she arrived, she stood at the edge of the beach and waited. From his ship, Ragnar saw her and called out, "What is your name, and what is your business here?"

Kraka replied:

I came at the command
Of Ragnar, captain and king;
I dared not deny his summons.
See now how I stand here
Both dressed and naked,
A net draped about my form,
And a fine friend at my side,
That I am not alone
Yet no man is with me.

Ragnar told two of his men to go and meet the young woman and bring her to the ship. Kraka said to the messengers when they arrived, "Gladly will I go to meet your captain and king, but only on condition that both I and my companion are guaranteed safety."

The messengers promised safe conduct to Kraka and the dog, and then led her onto the ship. But when Ragnar went to greet Kraka, the dog bit him. When Ragnar's men saw this, they jumped at the dog and killed it.

Kraka stayed on board for a time, conversing with Ragnar. Ragnar saw that Kraka was every bit as wise and clever as she was beautiful, and he longed to have her for his wife. Ragnar asked her to stay with him, but Kraka replied that if she truly had safe conduct, he would let her go in peace.

"Why will you not stay?" said Ragnar. "I am wholly pleased with you, and I love you. I wish you to stay here with me tonight and become my wife."

"I will not stay tonight," said Kraka. "I will not stay at all until you have made one more journey and returned to me in the same mind you are now. For it is possible that once you have sailed away, you will forget all about me, and had I wed you, I would be forsaken."

Ragnar was vexed that Kraka would not stay with him. He tried one last time to get her to stay by presenting her with a beautifully embroidered shirt that had belonged to his beloved Thora, which he carried with him wherever he went in her memory.

As he presented the shirt, Ragnar said:

Take this now, O maiden,

Glittering gift woven well

That once adorned my beloved Thora.

Sewn by her own hand

Have it now for your own!

Take this gift from a king and a captain

The dearest thing he can bestow.

Kraka replied:

A gracious gift indeed

And graciously given;

But not for the poor maid

Is the shimmering shirt of Thora.

More fitting is the coarse tunic

Blackened with soot.

Crow's-wing color[xciv]

Is what Kraka should wear

For herding the beasts

On paths high and low.

Lordly linen is not meet

For the poor man's daughter.

Then Kraka said, "I will now go home, and you will go on your errand. And if, when you return, you still desire me, send word to me, and I will come."

And so Kraka returned to the old couple's cottage, and Ragnar sailed with the first fair wind. After ten months, when Ragnar's journey was done, he returned to Spangarheith and sent his men to fetch Kraka, for he still desired her for his wife. Kraka agreed to go to Ragnar but not until the following morning.

Kraka arose very early. She went to the old couple and asked whether they were awake. When they said they were, Kraka said, "I am leaving, and I will never return. Listen now, for I have this to say to you: I know that you killed Heimer, my foster-father. I know that you stole the gold and the fine garments that he had hidden away, things that were rightfully mine. You have given me a roof over my head and clothes on my back, and although you have not been kind, you have done me no harm. Therefore I will not seek justice for what you have done. But I do wish one thing for you, that the remainder of your days be bad ones and each one worse than the last."

And so it was that Kraka returned to Ragnar's ship, where she was given a fair welcome. Ragnar sailed with Kraka and his men back to his homeland, where a great wedding feast was prepared. At the feast, Ragnar married Kraka and took him for his queen, and they lived many happy years together. Kraka gave Ragnar four fine sons who were named Ivar the Boneless, Björn Ironsides, Hvitserk, and Ragnvald. Ivar was called "the Boneless" because his bones were soft and did not knit properly.[xcv] He could not walk and had to be carried everywhere on a litter. What he lacked in physical strength he made up for in wisdom and cunning, and his brothers and stepbrothers all relied on his good counsel. Björn was named "Ironsides" because his skin was so tough that no weapon could penetrate it. Ragnvald died young, killed in battle in an attack on Whitby that Ivar had planned.

The Feud with King Eystein

There came a time when Ragnar went to visit King Eystein in Uppsala. Ragnar and Eystein were old friends and allies, and so there was much joy when they met at Eystein's court. Eystein had a beautiful daughter named Ingeborg, who had not yet been betrothed to any man. Now, Ragnar's advisers had long been vexed that their queen was the daughter of farmers, and when they saw how beautiful Ingeborg was, they began to speak out against Kraka in the hopes that Ragnar would divorce her and marry Ingeborg instead.

Ragnar had noted the beauty of Ingeborg, and he was swayed by the arguments of his advisers. Eystein also wished his daughter to marry Ragnar. When it came time to sail for home, Ragnar left Uppsala having promised to divorce Kraka and marry Ingeborg.

As Kraka waited at home for her husband to return, she sat in the courtyard under a tree working at some embroidery. While she worked, three birds came and sat in the branches of the tree. The birds then sang this song:

Queen and lady art thou now,

Until king and captain should break his vow

And a new bride place upon the throne.

His heart towards you he turns to stone.

And so it was that Kraka learned of Ragnar's plan to divorce her and marry another instead.[xcvi]

When Ragnar returned home, Kraka pretended that she knew nothing of his intent. She greeted him joyfully as she always did, asking how his visit had gone and how his friends fared. By this time, Ragnar was beginning to feel that he had behaved churlishly in agreeing to marry Ingeborg and put Kraka away, and because of his shame, he was very curt in his answers. This served only to confirm for Kraka what the birds had said to her. Finally Kraka decided to reveal what she knew.

"Why do you intend to divorce me and marry another?" asked Kraka.

"Who told you that?" said Ragnar, for only he and his closest advisers knew of this plan, and they had only just returned home.

"Three birds I have who are friendly to me. When you go on journeys, I send them to follow you so that they may bring me news. While I sat in the courtyard at my embroidery, they came and sang to me that you wish to have another woman in my place. Why would you want to do that? What ill have I done to you to make you wish to send me away?"

"No ill have you done, but your lowly birth counts against you," said Ragnar. "My advisers grow restless at having a peasant for a queen."

"Then tell your advisers that they are badly mistaken and that no peasant sits upon the throne but rather the daughter of Sigurd Fafnirsbane and the Valkyrie Brynhild," said Kraka. [xcvii] "You found me living among peasants, but those people are not my parents. When I was but a very small child, my foster-father, King Heimer, spirited me away from my father's court to keep me safe from the men who had killed my father. Heimer hid me inside his harp, along with some valuables, and took to the road in search of a place where we might live in peace.

"One day we came to Grima and Aki's farmstead, where Heimer asked for shelter. Grima and Aki killed my foster-father for the gold and fine garments he carried within his harp. When they broke open the harp to get at the valuable things, they also found me there. The old people adopted me and kept me as their own, but I am none of their blood. A daughter of the Volsungs am I, well fit to be your queen. My true name is Aslaug."

"An astonishing tale to be sure," said Ragnar, "but what proof have you that this is true? For proof I must have if I am to convince my advisers and if I am to break my betrothal to Ingeborg, daughter of King Eystein."

"Two things Grima and Aki allowed me to keep when they found me," said Aslaug. "One is my mother's wedding ring. The other is a letter my mother wrote to me before she died. Also, I have found myself again with child. When the child is born, it will be a boy, and he will have the image of a serpent in one of his eyes as a token of his relation to my father, who slew the great dragon Fafnir."

Aslaug then produced the ring and the letter, and when her time came to be delivered of her child, she gave birth to a boy who had the image of a serpent in one eye. The child was named Sigurd Snake-in-the Eye in honor of his grandfather and on account of the marking in his eye.

Ragnar saw all these tokens and begged forgiveness of Aslaug. Then he sent word to Eystein that he must break his betrothal to Ingeborg. And thus it was that Ragnar and Eystein, who had been friends from of old, became sworn enemies. This enmity would prove to be the undoing of Agnar and Erik, Ragnar's sons by his first wife, Thora.

When Ragnar went back on his promise to wed Ingeborg, Eystein vowed revenge. Eystein summoned his army with the intent of marching to Denmark and taking Ragnar's stronghold. As soon as word arrived of what Eystein purposed to do, Ragnar mustered his men and prepared to go to war, but Agnar and Erik asked to be sent at the head of the army in Ragnar's place.

"We are men full grown, Father," said Agnar. "Give us the honor of leading your army into battle. We lack nothing in strength or skill, and we wish only to return victorious as you have done many a time."

Ragnar gave his sons his blessing. Agnar and Erik went forth with Ragnar's army, and in time they met Eystein and his warriors as they were marching toward Denmark. There was a great and fierce battle. Agnar and Erik acquitted themselves well and slew many, but their army was thrown into disarray by an enchanted cow that Eystein loosed in their midst. Soon all was lost, for not only had Ragnar's army been thrown into confusion by the cow, but they were also overwhelmed by the greater numbers of warriors in Eystein's army.

When the battle was finally done, Agnar lay dead on the field, while Erik and a great part of Ragnar's army had been captured by Eystein.

"A bold and skilled warrior are you," Eystein said to Erik. "I would have peace between us. Take my daughter to wife, and you may stay here in my country. Great riches will be yours."

"No peace can there be between us," said Erik. "You slew my brother; I saw his body on the field. Keep your daughter, and keep your riches. All I ask is that my father's men be allowed to go home in safety and a nest of spears be planted in the ground for me that I may join my brother in death."

Eystein saw that Erik was not to be swayed, so he ordered that Ragnar's warriors be allowed to travel home unmolested and that a nest of spears be made with the shafts planted in the ground and the points facing upward. When the spears had been planted, Erik took the ring from his hand and gave it to one of his men. "Take this ring home to my stepmother," he said, "and tell her and my stepbrothers how the sons of Thora died." Then Erik threw himself upon the points of the spears and so perished.

When Ragnar heard what had happened in Sweden, he was enraged by the defeat of his army, and even more so by the deaths of his two eldest sons. Aslaug likewise mourned Agnar and Erik as though they had been her own. Ivar and Björn went before their father and begged his blessing to go to Sweden and avenge their stepbrothers' deaths. Ragnar gladly granted them leave, and so they sailed with the next fair wind, having assembled a great body of picked warriors known for their courage and skill.

When the day of the battle arrived, Eystein once again loosed his enchanted cow into the ranks of Ragnar's men. Again the army was thrown into disarray, but Ivar was not dismayed. Although Ivar could not walk, he was still a redoubtable archer, and in this battle, he showed both his skill and his coolheadedness. As the enchanted cow plunged up and down, scattering Ragnar's warriors, Ivar fitted an arrow to the string and loosed a deadly shot, killing the cow instantly. Once the cow's enchantment had been dispelled, Ragnar's men rallied. Soon the Swedish warriors were put to flight, and Eystein was killed as he ran away from the field. Thus were the sons of Thora and Ragnar Lodbrok avenged.

The Death of Ragnar Lothbrok

When the battle with Eystein was over, Ragnar's remaining sons took ship and went raiding. They sailed southward, capturing town after town and laying waste to village after village. Finally they reached the central coast of Italy, where they thought to raid a city called Luna. They beached their ships within view of the town, and all the townsfolk scurried to secure their gates and garrison their walls in expectation of a Viking assault.

Now, the captain of the Viking ships was a man named Hastein, who was both clever and a skilled warrior, well trusted by Ragnar's sons, and foster-father to Sigurd Snake-in-the-Eye. When the Vikings saw that Luna was too well defended to capture by a direct attack, Hastein came up with a cunning plan instead. Messengers were sent into the town with instructions to say that the Vikings had no intention of raiding. They told the leaders of the town and its church that their captain, a man named Hastein, had fallen gravely ill and wished to be baptized as a Christian before he died. A priest was dispatched to the Viking ships in order to give the sacrament to Hastein, who pretended to be fully converted and to accept Christ as his god.

A few days after Hastein's supposed conversion, the Vikings sent word to the town saying that their captain had died. They told the town leaders that Hastein wished for a funeral Mass with Christian burial and that he had left all his fortune to the church in Luna. Thinking that since the Vikings had not yet shown any wish to attack the town they would continue to behave peacefully, the governor of the town gave leave to the Vikings to bring Hastein's coffin into the city gates and to attend the funeral Mass.

Little did the governor know that Hastein was fully alive inside his coffin and that the Vikings had no intention of leaving without plundering the town. In accord with Hastein's plan, the Vikings made a grand funeral procession into the church, where Hastein's coffin was laid upon a bier. But once the church doors were closed and the Mass began, Hastein kicked open the coffin and sprang out, sword drawn. The other Vikings drew the weapons they had concealed within their clothing, and thus they slew all the worthies of the town. Then they ran out of the church to sack and set fire to the houses.

After the sack of Luna, Ragnar's sons laid waste to many other towns. Soon word of their exploits was carried back to Ragnar's court.

"I must take ship again," Ragnar said. "I will have no one say that Ragnar's sons are more valiant than their father."

Now, many years ago, Ragnar had invaded England and made devastating raids all through the country. Ragnar had demanded tribute from the king as the price of peace, but once Ragnar sailed home, the king had refused to pay it. Ragnar deemed an expedition to exact the tribute to be a chance for glory that would rival that of his sons, and so he caused two ships to be made, each large enough to carry a great host. When Aslaug saw what Ragnar was doing, she feared for the success of his raid. "Husband," she said, "would it not be better to sail with many smaller ships rather than two large ones?"

"Perhaps," Ragnar answered, "but no man has ever conquered England with only two ships, and I mean to be the first one to do it. Think of the songs that will be sung! My fame will be everlasting."

Aslaug tried and tried to sway her husband, but Ragnar stood firm. Finally Aslaug realized it was futile to argue with him. She went to the chest where she kept her dearest treasures, and from it she took a magic shirt that she had woven from her own hair and that had been made without any seams.

"Since your course is not to be altered, take this shirt with you," said Aslaug. "Wear it into battle. It will protect you from all wounds, and then maybe you will be able to return home to me."

When the ships were made and provisioned and the army assembled, Ragnar sailed for England, but his voyage was ill-fated from the start. As Ragnar's ships approached the coast, a great storm blew up, and the ships foundered on the rocks not far from the beach. Undaunted, Ragnar and his men made their way onto land, where they began raiding every village and hamlet that stood in their path.

Word of the Viking attacks came to King Ella. He assembled a great host and went out to meet Ragnar's army, intending to crush it thoroughly before it could do any more damage. The English had the greater host by far, so the battle was decided quickly in Ella's favor. Most of Ragnar's men were killed, and Ragnar himself was taken prisoner.

Ragnar was bound and taken before the king. "Tell us your name and your station," Ella demanded, but Ragnar refused to answer.

"If you will not answer," said Ella, "you will be thrown into a pit of venomous serpents. I ask you again: what is your name and your station?"

Ragnar kept his silence, so Ella did as he said he would do. Ragnar was taken and thrown into a deep pit in which there were many venomous snakes.[xcviii] The snakes tried to bite Ragnar, but they were not able to pierce his skin because of the magic shirt Aslaug had given him. When the English realized why Ragnar was not yet dying, they stripped the shirt from him and left him to his fate.

Without the shirt, the serpents were able to sink their fangs into Ragnar's flesh. Soon Ragnar felt the venom coursing through his veins and knew his death was very near. As he was dying, Ragnar sang his death-song:

Battles fifty and one fought I.

Fearless, dauntless, countless foes I have slain;

My sword shone red with their blood

And the dragon feared my spear-point.

Now death deals its blow to me,

My bane not battle-borne but a writhing worm.

Now Valhalla awaits, the warrior's paradise;

Odin-sent Valkyries descend to take me home.

How the sons of Aslaug will rage

When they find how their hero-father met his doom.

Odin calls me now, ale-cups brimful in his halls.

Dying I sing the song of my deeds;

I laugh as life drains away.[xcix]

When Ella heard Ragnar sing of the sons of Aslaug, he realized who it was that had been thrown into the pit. He ordered Ragnar to be taken out with all haste, hoping that it would be possible to save him and thus avoid the wrath of his sons, but it was too late. Ragnar was already dead by the time his body was brought up out of the pit. Thus ended the life of Ragnar Lothbrok, king, hero, and dragon's bane.

The Revenge of Ragnar's Sons

Now that Ragnar Lothbrok was dead, Ella sent messengers to inform Ragnar's sons. "Mark well how each one takes the news," said Ella, "and bring that information back to me."

Ragnar's sons had arrived home from their own voyaging while their father was away in England. The messenger found the young men taking their ease in the great hall of Ragnar's stronghold. Ivar sat on Ragnar's throne, while Hvitserk and Sigurd played chess. Björn also was there, whittling a spear shaft so that a head might be fitted to it.

As the messenger told the tale of Ragnar's last battle, of his death in the snake pit, and of his last song, Ivar sat cold and unmoving on the throne, listening to every detail and occasionally asking questions of the messenger. The only sign of Ivar's distress was the change of color in his cheeks, which shifted from pallor to redness. Björn, however, grasped the spear shaft in his hands and broke it in two. Hvitserk picked up a chess piece and squeezed it in his hand so hard that the piece shattered and his nails were driven into the flesh, drawing blood. Sigurd, who had been paring his nails with a knife, paid no attention to what he was doing with the blade and so cut his finger to the bone.

When the messenger was done with his tale, Björn said, "Strike down this dog where he stands. No man should live who has seen the death of Ragnar Lothbrok."

"Stay, Björn," said Ivar. "The messenger came in peace, having been sent by his king. He has done his duty, and now he will be allowed to return home in peace."

The messenger left Ragnar's court and returned to England, where he told Ella all that had happened while he delivered his message.

"Ivar is the one we have to fear," said Ella once he had heard all, "although the others surely are dangerous enough in their own right. Set a guard on our eastern coast, and bring news with all speed if Viking sails are on the horizon."

At Ragnar's court, the brothers debated what was to be done.

"Let us take ship with every man who can bear arms and teach Ella a lesson he will not forget!" said Hvitserk.

"Yes, indeed!" said Björn. "We must have vengeance, and Ella will pay with his blood and the blood of many others besides!"

"Yes, Ella must pay," said Ivar, "but why not ask of him wergild and be done?" Ragnar was told at the time of his sailing that leaving with only two ships was folly, and now he has suffered the fate that was foretold. Why should more good men die for Ragnar's ill choices?"

"Wergild is the coward's vengeance," said Sigurd. "I agree with Hvitserk and Björn. Let us take ship and sail for England as soon as may be."

In the end, the brothers took ship with as many warriors as they could muster. Ivar went along with them, but he refused to take part in the battle. The battle was quickly decided in Ella's favor, and Hvitserk, Björn, and Sigurd were taken captive.

When Ivar learned of the course of the battle and his brothers' fates, he went before Ella to plead for their release. "In recompense for the death of our father, let my brothers return home in safety," said Ivar, "and also give me a small wergild: the amount of land that I might compass within an oxhide. I will remain here in England, and I vow never to take arms against you while I live."

Ella agreed to these terms, thinking the wergild Ivar requested to be both odd and so small as to be laughable, although he did not say so at the time. Hvitserk, Björn, and Sigurd sailed home, while Ivar remained behind in England. Ivar did indeed take a piece of land encompassed by an oxhide, but when Ivar had finished placing the hide, Ella was no longer laughing. Crafty Ivar took the oxhide and had it made soft and pliable, then stretched it out to its greatest extent. When the hide was well stretched, he cut it into the thinnest of strips. Then he took the strips and sewed them end on end in a great circle. Ivar took the circle of oxhide and placed it around a large piece of land, on which he built a stronghold and founded a town called Lundunaborg.[ci]

Ivar managed his affairs well and befriended all of the nobles in the lands around, treating them even better at his own court than they had been at Ella's. Ivar also pretended to be at peace with Ella and acted toward him as a willing friend and adviser. Soon Ella had been soothed into complacency and Ivar had a great many well-placed friends who were ripe for rebellion. Ivar urged the English nobles to rise up and take the throne from Ella, for Ivar had never forgiven the king for Ragnar's death, and he still intended to make Ella pay dearly for it.

Once all was ready, Ivar sent word to his brothers to muster their armies and sail for England. The brothers and their warriors arrived, and with the aid of Ivar's English friends, they brought battle to Ella. Ella's army was caught by surprise, and its numbers had been badly depleted by the defection of so many nobles. Ella himself was captured and put to death by having the image of an eagle in flight carved into his back with a knife.[cii]

Their vengeance accomplished, Hvitserk, Björn, and Sigurd returned home and divided their father's kingdom among them. Björn took the parts that were in Sweden, while Sigurd ruled in Denmark. Hvitserk continued to sail on voyages, looking for plunder, until he was taken captive and executed. Ivar remained in England, where he had established a Viking colony in Northumbria.

Thus ends the saga of Ragnar Lothbrok and his sons.

Notes to The Saga of Ragnar Lothbrok and His Sons

Kirsten Wolf, *Daily Life of the Vikings* (Westport: The Greenwood Press, 2004), p. 22.

[1] Wolf, *Daily Life*, p. 22.

[1] Wolf, *Daily Life*, p. 22.

[1] Richard Hall, *The World of the Vikings* (New York: Thames and Hudson, 2007), pp. 40-43.

[1] Anders Winroth, *The Age of the Vikings* (Princeton: Princeton University Press, 2014), pp. 138-9.

[1] James Graham-Campbell, ed., *Cultural Atlas of the Viking World* (Oxford: Andromeda, 1994), p. 63.

[1] Graham-Campbell, *Cultural Atlas*, pp. 80-83.

[1] Wolf, *Daily Life*, p. 8.

[1] Wolf, *Daily Life*, pp. 10-11.

[1] Wolf, *Daily Life*, pp. 22-24.

[1] Winroth, *Age of the Vikings*, pp. 164-65.

[1] The stories of women warriors in Saxo's history are summarized in Judith Jesch, *Women in the Viking Age* (Woodbridge: The Boydell Press, 1991), pp. 176ff.

[1] Charlotte Hendenstierna-Jonson et al., "A Female Viking Warrior Confirmed by Genomics," *American Journal of Physical Anthropology* 164/4 (2017): 853-60.

[1] Hendenstierna-Jonson et al., "Female Viking Warrior," p. 855.

[1] Hendenstierna-Jonson et al., "Female Viking Warrior," p. 855-57.

[1] Hall, *World of the Vikings*, p. 34.

[1] Jesch, *Women in the Viking Age*, pp. 183-85.

[1] Wolf, *Daily Life*, p. 13.

[1] Wolf, *Daily Life*, pp. 8-9.

[1] Wolf, *Daily Life*, p. 10.

[1] Wolf, *Daily Life*, p. 10.

[1] Winroth, *Age of the Vikings*, pp. 162-64.

[1] Winroth, *Age of the Vikings*, pp. 162-64.

[1] Winroth, *Age of the Vikings*, pp. 163-64.

[1] Neil Oliver, *The Vikings: A New History* (New York: Pegasus Books LLC, 2013), p. 108.

[1] Winroth, *Age of the Vikings*, p. 123.

[1] John Haywood, *Northmen: The Viking Saga AD 793-1241* (New York: St. Martin's Press, 2015), p. 14.

[1] Wolf, *Daily Life*, p. 24; Graham-Campbell, *Cultural Atlas*, p. 75.

[1] Haywood, *Northmen*, pp. 20-22; Graham-Campbell, *Cultural Atlas*, p. 75.

[1] Haywood, *Northmen*, p. 22.

[1] Graham-Campbell, *Cultural Atlas*, p. 75.

[1] Graham-Campbell, *Cultural Atlas*, p. 79.

[1] Wolf, *Daily Life*, p. 24.

[1] Graham-Campbell, *Cultural Atlas*, p. 78.

[1] Graham-Campbell, *Cultural Atlas*, p. 78.

[1] Hall, *World of the Vikings*, pp. 33, 99.

[1] Hall, *World of the Vikings*, p. 101.

[1] Hall, *World of the Vikings*, p. 101.

[1] Winroth, *Age of the Vikings*, pp. 124-27,

[1] Graham-Campbell, *Cultural Atlas*, p. 78.

[1] Graham-Campbell, *Cultural Atlas*, p. 85.

[1] Hall, *World of the Vikings*, p. 59.

[1] Hall, *World of the Vikings*, p. 60.

[1] Hall, *World of the Vikings*, p. 60. Ribe is a town in Denmark.

[1] Haywood, *Northmen*, pp. 42-3.

[1] Haywood, *Northmen*, p. 45.

[1] Haywood, *Northmen*, pp. 45, 88.

[1] Haywood, *Northmen*, pp. 169-70.

[1] Haywood, *Northmen*, p. 40.

[1] Winroth, *Age of the Vikings*, p. 136.

[1] Winroth, *Age of the Vikings*, pp. 136-39.

[1] Winroth, *Age of the Vikings*, pp. 136-37.

[1] Oliver, *New History*, pp. 99-100.

[1] Hall, *Vikings*, p. 54.

[1] Winroth, *Age of the Vikings*, p. 75.

[1] Haywood, *Northmen*, p. 47.

[1] Haywood, *Northmen*, p. 50.

[1] Oliver, New History, p. 169.

[1] Caroline Taggart, *The Book of English Place Names: How Our Towns and Villages Got Their Names* (n. p.: Ebury Press, 2011), pp. 15, 82, 269.

[1] Graham-Campbell, *Cultural Atlas*, pp. 190-91; Winroth, *Age of the Vikings*, p. 114.

[1] Graham-Campbell, *Cultural Atlas*, pp. 190-91.

[1] Graham-Campbell, *Cultural Atlas*, p. 192; Hall, *Vikings*, p. 97.

[1] Hall, *Vikings*, pp. 150, 152.

[1] Hall, *Vikings,* p. 151.

[1] Hall, *Vikings*, p. 181.

[1] Hall, *Vikings*, p. 160.

[1] Hall, *Vikings*, p. 161.

[1] Ben Waggoner, trans., *The Sagas of Ragnar Lodbrok* (New Haven: The Troth, 2009), p. xiii.

[1] Waggoner, *Sagas of Ragnar Lodbrok*, p. xi.

[1] Waggoner, *Sagas of Ragnar Lodbrok*, p. xiii.

[1] Waggoner, *Sagas of Ragnar Lodbrok*, p. xxiv. The manuscript in question is Copenhagen, Royal Danish Library, MS NkS 1824b 4to.

[1] This manuscript is Copenhagen, Royal Danish Library, MS AM 147 4to. Waggoner, *Sagas of Ragnar Lodbrok*, p. xxiv.

[1] Waggoner, *Sagas of Ragnar Lodbrok*, p. xxv. Waggoner also notes that the *Hauksbók* was broken up into its constituent pieces, and the pieces were rebound and catalogued separately. The portion containing the *Tale of Ragnar's Sons* now resides in the Arnamagnaean Institute at the University of Copenhagan as MS AM 544.

[1] Robert Crawford, *Scotland's Books: A History of Scottish Literature* (Oxford: Oxford University Press, 2009), n. p., accessed through Google Books <http://google.com/books> 23 March 2020.

[1] n. a., "Teutonic Forms," p. 3 (PDF accessed via https://www.jsicmail.ac.uk, 23 March 2020). The PDF appears to cite Turville-Petre, p. xix, as a source for the definition of *háttlausa* but does not give a bibliographical description beyond the author's surname and page number. It is possible that this information was taken from *Scaldic Poetry* by Gabriel Turville-Petre (Oxford: Clarendon Press, 1976), p. xxix, but I do not have access to this volume and so cannot confirm the accuracy of this assumption.

[1] Waggoner, *Sagas of Ragnar Lodbrok*, p. x.

[1] Oliver Elton, trans. *The Nine Books of the Danish History of Saxo Grammaticus.* 2 vols. (London: Norroena Society, [1905]).

[1] Elton, trans., *Saxo Grammaticus*, vol. 2, pp. 544–5.

[1] Elton, trans., *Saxo Grammaticus*, vol. 2, pp. 550 (Charlemagne episode) and 552–4 (Hellespont episode).

[1] Winroth, *Age of the Vikings*, pp. 134–38.

[1] Wolf, *Daily Life*, p. 55.

[1] Wolf, *Daily Life*, p. 55.

[1] Crawford, *Volsungs,* p. xv.

[1] R. Bartlett, "The Viking Hiatus in the Cult of Saints as Seen in the Twelfth Century," in *The Long Twelfth-Century View of the Anglo-Saxon Past,* edited by Martin Brett and David A. Woodman (Abingdon: Routledge, 2016), p. 18. Bartlett cites the F manuscript of the *Chronicle*, f. 54. "Viking Hiatus," n. 16.

[1] Bartlett, "Viking Hiatus," pp. 17–8.

[1] Bartlett, "Viking Hiatus," p. 18.

[1] Waggoner, *Sagas of Ragnar Lodbrok*, pp. xvi–xvii.

[1] Crawford, *Volsungs,* p. xix.

[1] Albert Welles, *The Pedigree and History of the Washington Family* (New York: Society Library, 1879).

[1] Welles, *Washington*, p. iv.

[1] In one medieval version of the saga, Ragnar states that he is fifteen years old in his verse to Thora, but this version does not include Ragnar's sojourn with Lagertha. Because I am including the story about Ragnar meeting and marrying Lagertha prior to his encounter with the dragon, I have changed Ragnar's age to eighteen to take his three years with Lagertha into account.

[1] A kenning for "dragon."

[1] Another kenning for "dragon."

[1] A kenning for "black." This is also a play on the name "Kraka," which itself means "crow."

[1] The original sources are unclear about what the exact nature of Ivar's disability was. In some ways, the descriptions seem to suggest a milder form of brittle bone disease (*osteogenesis imperfecta*), but they could also refer to rickets. Rickets is a childhood ailment that leads to a softening of the bones, which is caused by a lack of vitamin D. Effects of this softening include bow-leggedness and knock knees, which impairs one's ability to walk. Rickets is more common in northern latitudes because of the lack of sunlight during a significant part of the year. It can also be caused by genetic factors or by the mother having a severe vitamin D deficiency during pregnancy.

[1] Kraka/Aslaug's father also had the ability to understand the speech of birds, which he acquired by accidentally tasting some of the dragon Fafnir's blood while roasting its heart for Regin, the blacksmith to whom Sigurd was apprenticed and who was the brother of Fafnir.

[1] "Fafnirsbane" means "Killer of Fafnir."

[1] Although the saga was only written down in Christian times, one wonders whether the pit of snakes was intended to be some kind of reference to the pagan concept either of Hvergelmir or of Nastrandir. The latter was a place in the Norse underworld that was made out of venomous serpents, and the former was a place inhabited by a giant serpent. Nastrandir was the place to which the souls of oathbreakers and murderers were consigned and Hvergelmir the place where the

souls of the most wicked were consumed by the giant serpent. If this coincidence of imagery between pagan beliefs and the saga's text were in fact intended, it may add yet more degradation to the method used for Ragnar's death since it signals that Ella finds him to be not a noble enemy but rather a dishonorable murderer. It is also possible that a link was intended to be made between Ragnar and Gunnar from the *Saga of the Volsungs*, who also meets his end in a pit of snakes.

[1] This is a significantly shortened version of the *Krákumál*, a 29-stave poem purported to be Ragnar's death-song. In fact, the *Krákumál* is a twelfth-century creation, probably written somewhere in the Scottish islands.

[1] Payment of wergild was an important practice in ancient Germanic and Scandinavian societies. The purpose of wergild was to compensate a victim—or the victim's family, if the victim had been killed—for the hurt they had received through the perpetrator's commission of a crime. The amount to be paid varied depending on the nature of the injury and the gender and social status of the parties concerned. Once wergild had been paid, the victim and/or their family had to relinquish any right to exact further payment or vengeance.

[1] Some of the sources I consulted said that "Lundunaborg" was London; others said that it was Lincoln. Neither identification can be historically accurate since both London and Lincoln were founded by the Romans long before the Vikings ever arrived in England. Peter Munch is in the "London" camp in his *Norse Mythology: Legends of Gods and Heroes* (New York: American-Scandinavian Foundation, 1926), p. 251. Katharine F. Boult, on the other hand, claims that Ivar's stronghold was Lincoln. *Asgard & the Norse Heroes* (London: J. M. Dent & Sons, Ltd., [1914]), p. 253.

[1] The medieval sources do not agree on exactly what Ella's torture and death entailed. Some seem to indicate that the image of an eagle was carved into his back, but another version states that the "eagle" was created by cracking open the victim's rib cage from the back and

then splaying his lungs out as though they were wings. Historian Anders Winroth says that the difficulty in translating the original Old Norse has led to other misunderstandings of the "blood eagle." Winroth says that the interpretation in which an eagle is carved into Ella's back with a knife likewise may be a mistranslation, although he finds it grammatically correct, and that it might have been the saga creator's original intent to say that Ella was killed and then his body left as food for birds of prey. *The Age of the Vikings* (Princeton: Princeton University Press, 2014), pp. 36-7.

Part III: Representations of Norse Myths and History in Modern Media

Dragons in Tolkien's Middle-Earth

J. R. R. Tolkien's *The Lord of the Rings* and *The Hobbit, or There and Back Again* have captured the imaginations of readers since their initial publication in the middle of the twentieth century, and have been brought to an even wider audience by Peter Jackson's recent film adaptations. Tolkien's voluminous writings about Middle-earth, its history, and its inhabitants opened up new worlds for generations of his fans and inspired many other writers.

Just as Tolkien's writings became a spur for creators who followed him, ancient Norse and Anglo-Saxon myths were among Tolkien's own inspirations and are deeply woven into his fiction. Tolkien did not generally distance himself from his sources; rather, he was happy to claim that "[i]n the Lord of the Rings, I have tried to modernize the myths and make them credible."[ciii]

Tolkien's exposure both to ancient Norse myths and to Anglo-Saxon literature came early in his life, as did his interest in constructed languages. When Tolkien was a young child, he read Andrew Lang's version of the *Saga of the Volsungs* in the *Red Fairy Book*, and around the same time, he made his first experiments with constructed languages.[civ] In his teens, Tolkien was a pupil at King Edward's School in Birmingham, where he studied Anglo-Saxon and began teaching himself to read Old Norse.[cv] Old Norse became his special subject in his undergraduate studies at Oxford, as an adjunct to his primary concentration, which was on a linguistic study of English.[cvi]

This interest in languages and Norse and Anglo-Saxon literature alike would create the arc of Tolkien's professional life, the bulk of which was spent at Oxford University, where he was the Rawlinson and Bosworth Professor of Anglo-Saxon and a Fellow of Pembroke College between 1925 and 1945, while from 1945 to 1959 he was the Merton Professor of English Language and Literature and a Fellow of Merton College.[cvii] It was during his tenure at Oxford and in his retirement thereafter that Tolkien wrote *The Hobbit, The Lord of the Rings*, and other tales set in Middle-earth, the last of which were published by Tolkien's son, Christopher, after the elder Tolkien's death in 1973.

The connections between Tolkien's works and Norse mythology are complex and extensive enough to fill a book of their own, so I am going to narrow my focus to the matter of dragons in these two bodies of literature. Just as dragons are important figures in *Beowulf* and in the Icelandic sagas, including Ragnar's own, so too do they abound in Tolkien's works, from the terrifying Ancalagon the Black and the deadly, wingless Glaurung in *The Silmarillion*, to glittering Smaug in *The Hobbit*, to the wheedling, clever, cowardly Chrysophylax the Rich of "Farmer Giles of Ham," a humorous short story set not in the fantasy realm of Middle-earth but rather in an imagined medieval England. It should be no surprise to find that Tolkien himself admitted that when he was a child, he "desired dragons with a profound desire."[cviii]

Although all of Tolkien's dragons are worthy of further discussion, I will concentrate on the parallels between Fafnir in the *Saga of the*

Volsungs, on the one hand, and Smaug and Glaurung in Tolkien's books *The Hobbit* and *The Silmarillion*, respectively, on the other. Bilbo's interaction with Smaug in *The Hobbit* also has resonances with the Anglo-Saxon epic poem *Beowulf*, and there are two small points of resemblance between Glaurung in *The Silmarillion* and the unnamed dragon in the *Saga of Ragnar Lothbrok*.

Author Jonathan Evans notes some parallels between Smaug, the dragon in *The Hobbit*, and the dragon in the last part of *Beowulf* in the events that trigger their rampages. In both stories, the dragons become enraged over the loss of one small cup from each of their hoards.[cix] Bilbo takes the cup in *The Hobbit* during his first visit to Smaug's lair, while in *Beowulf* the item is stolen by a man who goes unnamed.[cx]

The manner of Smaug's death comes from a different source, instead echoing Sigurd's slaying of the dragon Fafnir in the *Saga of the Volsungs*. In both stories, the dragon is brought low by a weapon piercing a weak spot in the underbelly near the left shoulder. Fafnir dies from a sword thrust given by Sigurd, who hides in a pit and attacks the dragon as he passes overhead, while Smaug is killed by an arrow shot by a Lakeman named Bard.[cxi]

In each case, the person killing the dragon is given advice on how to go about it. In *Volsungs*, Sigurd's foster-father, Regin, tells Sigurd to dig and hide in a pit and to stab the dragon as it passes overhead. As Sigurd is digging, Odin, appearing in the guise of an old, one-eyed man, tells Sigurd to dig multiple pits to protect himself from being overwhelmed by the flow of the dragon's blood. In *The Hobbit*, a thrush that has been hanging around the dwarves' camp overhears Bilbo telling the dwarves about the weakness he observed when he first entered the dragon's lair.[cxii] The thrush then carries this information to the Lakeman Bard.[cxiii] Bard's ability to understand the speech of birds also recalls *Volsungs*: Sigurd gains that same ability when he accidentally tastes some of Fafnir's blood after killing him, and the birds' speech to one another saves Sigurd's life just as the thrush saves Bard's, by warning Sigurd that his foster-father, Regin, intends to kill him.[cxiv]

As in *The Hobbit,* Tolkien appropriates some details from Sigurd's story in the *Saga of the Volsungs* for reuse in the story of Turin Turambar in *The Silmarillion.* Some of these are small elements: for example, both Turin and Sigurd wear dragon-helms and wield twice-forged swords, and both suffer unhappy fates. Here, however, I would like to concentrate on each hero's interactions with the dragons they slay. For Sigurd, this is Fafnir, while for Turin, this is Glaurung, the first dragon created in Middle-earth through the power of Morgoth, the Dark Lord.

As we have seen, Sigurd slays Fafnir with a sword thrust from below. Turin does the same in his final encounter with Glaurung but with rather more risk to Turin, who instead of waiting in relative safety inside a pit, climbs a cliff on one side of a chasm to await the dragon as it passes over the gap between the place where Turin waits and the other side.

The final scene including both Turin and Glaurung also has some resonances with the *Saga of Ragnar Lothbrok.* Ragnar gains the nickname "Lothbrok," or "shaggy breeches," because of the suit he makes to protect himself from the venom and blood of the dragon. The suit is effective: when some of the dying dragon's blood splashes on Ragnar, he is unhurt. Turin, on the other hand, is not as lucky or perhaps not as foresighted as Ragnar. When Turin pulls his sword out of Glaurung's side, the dragon's blood gushes out, and some lands on Turin's hand, burning it. And like the dragon in Ragnar's story, Glaurung has no wings.

The characters of Fafnir, Smaug, and Glaurung themselves also have some things in common, especially in the ways in which they relate to Sigurd, Bilbo, and Turin, respectively. Tolkien takes these commonalities and molds them somewhat differently for Smaug than he does for Glaurung, partly because of the tone of each of these stories. The story of Turin Turambar is both a tragedy and also a romance in the medieval sense of the word, having been written in a deliberately archaic voice intended to evoke the sense that what one is reading is a document from an ancient past, not something created by a twentieth-century Oxford don. *The Hobbit*, by contrast, for all its battles, giant spiders, goblins, and dragons, was written for children and so maintains a fairly lighthearted tone.

Unlike the dragon in Ragnar's saga, who remains silent throughout his encounter with Ragnar, Fafnir and Tolkien's dragons speak to the heroes of their respective stories. After Sigurd gives Fafnir his death blow, Fafnir asks, "Who is thy father, and what thy race?" Sigurd answers, "My race is unknown to men; I am called the Noble Beast, and I have no father or mother, for I have journeyed alone."[cxv] In the conversation that follows, Sigurd reveals his true name and endures a series of slights by the dragon followed by an exchange about death and fate before Fafnir curses his treasure and then dies.

In this conversation, Sigurd and Fafnir relate to one another more or less as equals. They ask and answer one another's questions, and although Fafnir tries to frighten Sigurd with dire portents to follow if Sigurd touches Fafnir's treasure, the dragon does not seem to think of Sigurd as being somehow beneath him.

Glaurung, by contrast, is openly contemptuous of Turin. The dragon insults Turin, much as Fafnir does Sigurd, but Glaurung's taunts are significantly more venomous. At their first meeting, Glaurung does not kill Turin; he instead wounds the hero psychologically and emotionally by calling him "[t]hankless fosterling, outlaw, slayer of thy friend, thief of love, usurper of Nargothrond, captain foolhardy and deserter of thy kin."[cxvi] Now, all of these things are technically true and are descriptions of actual events from Turin's life, but Glaurung is using them and the insults against Turin's family that follow to make Turin doubt himself and thus weaken him in the fight against Glaurung's creator, Morgoth. Although Turin then attempts to attack Glaurung, the dragon simply dodges out of the way and then slithers off while making further taunts, apparently thinking he has already wasted too much time and effort on this puny man who is beneath his notice.[cxvii]

Another exchange takes place later in the story, this time between Glaurung and Nienor, Turin's wife, as Glaurung is dying. Glaurung mocks Nienor with the news that she is actually Turin's sister—a fact of which neither Nienor nor Turin were aware—after which Glaurung denigrates Turin yet again before dying.[cxviii] Not long afterward, Turin learns that his mother has died and that Nienor has lost her memory and run away.[cxix] Exhausted and bereft, Turin kills himself by throwing himself onto the blade of his sword.[cxx]

Tolkien takes Sigurd's interaction with Fafnir and uses it as the model for Glaurung's conversations with Turin and Nienor but expands on his model by creating three encounters instead of one involving not one but two characters. Tolkien also heightens the emotional stakes by making Glaurung's speeches to Turin and Nienor even more cruel than Fafnir's to Sigurd, as well as by elevating the dragon's malice toward the humans he torments.

In *The Hobbit*, by contrast, Tolkien instead takes the riddling part of Sigurd's conversation with Fafnir as the model for Bilbo's interaction with Smaug, increasing the number of riddles and using the conversation as an opportunity for Smaug to gloat over his superiority to the puny thief who dares confront him and touch even the smallest item of his treasure. Unlike Glaurung's gloating and taunts, which become the undoing both of Turin and of Nienor, Smaug's insults hold the seeds of his own destruction: he boasts about his gem-encrusted underbelly and then shows it to Bilbo, who spies the one bald patch on the left side that will become the dragon's bane. Further, Bilbo's more or less successful riddling shows the courage and sharp wits of the little Hobbit who, only a few months earlier, was "kneeling on the hearth-rug, shaking like a jelly that was melting" at the suggestion he would be going on a serious adventure with Gandalf and the Dwarves.[cxxi] Unlike Turin, Bilbo comes away emboldened from his encounter with a dragon.

Like Bilbo, Sigurd begins his interaction with Fafnir by concealing his identity within a series of riddles, but Sigurd quickly gives up the pretense when Fafnir insists he tell the truth. Sigurd does, not least because he knows the dragon is dying and won't be able to come after him later. Bilbo, however, has no such assurances since Smaug is very much alive, and there is no guarantee that he will be destroyed. Also, while Sigurd treats Fafnir more or less as a defeated peer, Bilbo, by contrast, realizes how very small and powerless he is—with which Smaug obviously agrees—and so addresses the dragon by flattering titles such as "Smaug the Tremendous" and "Smaug the Chiefest and Greatest of Calamities."[cxxii]

When Smaug asks who Bilbo is and where he comes from, Bilbo replies with a series of riddles that refer obliquely both to his origins and to the adventures he has had up to this point:

> I come from under the hill, and under the hills and over the hills my paths led. And through the air. I am he that walks unseen.... I am the clue-finder, the web-cutter, the stinging fly. I was chosen for the lucky number.... I am he that buries his friends alive and drowns them and draws them alive again from the water. I came from the end of a bag, but no bag went over me.... I am the friend of bears and the guest of eagles. I am Ringwinner and Luckwearer; and I am Barrel-rider.[cxxiii]

After this bit of dialogue, Tolkien goes on to give the reader some instruction in interacting with dragons, noting that it is wise to hide one's name but unwise to refuse to answer at all, and that therefore Bilbo is doing very well indeed in this extraordinarily dangerous situation. Tolkien then explains why it is a good idea to approach dragons this way, saying that "[n]o dragon can resist the fascination of riddling talk and of wasting time trying to understand it."[cxxiv]

This is true of Fafnir just as it is true of Smaug: as Fafnir is dying, he tries to work out the riddle of Sigurd's identity, which is then followed by a series of questions and answers about the nature of the Norns, the goddesses who determine the fates of all human beings, and the dwelling place of the fire god Surt, before Fafnir goes on to warn Sigurd about the doom that will be upon him if he touches Fafnir's gold.[cxxv]

In his own fiction, Tolkien took the Norse stories he so deeply loved and which he knew so intimately and used them as inspiration for new characters and events. But instead of copying what he found in the sagas, Tolkien reworked them, adapting them to his own ends and making them rich elements on which to base fresh stories, stories for readers who, like Tolkien, desire dragons with a profound desire.

Notes to "Dragons in Tolkien's Middle-Earth"

Kirsten Wolf, *Daily Life of the Vikings* (Westport: The Greenwood Press, 2004), p. 22.

[1] Wolf, *Daily Life*, p. 22.

[1] Wolf, *Daily Life*, p. 22.

[1] Richard Hall, *The World of the Vikings* (New York: Thames and Hudson, 2007), pp. 40–43.

[1] Anders Winroth, *The Age of the Vikings* (Princeton: Princeton University Press, 2014), pp. 138–9.

[1] James Graham-Campbell, ed., *Cultural Atlas of the Viking World* (Oxford: Andromeda, 1994), p. 63.

[1] Graham-Campbell, *Cultural Atlas*, pp. 80–83.

[1] Wolf, *Daily Life*, p. 8.

[1] Wolf, *Daily Life*, pp. 10–11.

[1] Wolf, *Daily Life*, pp. 22–24.

[1] Winroth, *Age of the Vikings*, pp. 164–65.

The stories of women warriors in Saxo's history are summarized in Judith Jesch, *Women in the Viking Age* (Woodbridge: The Boydell Press, 1991), pp. 176ff.

Charlotte Hendenstierna-Jonson et al., "A Female Viking Warrior Confirmed by Genomics," *American Journal of Physical Anthropology* 164/4 (2017): 853-60.

Hendenstierna-Jonson et al., "Female Viking Warrior," p. 855.

Hendenstierna-Jonson et al., "Female Viking Warrior," p. 855-57.

Hall, *World of the Vikings*, p. 34.

Jesch, *Women in the Viking Age*, pp. 183-85.

Wolf, *Daily Life*, p. 13.

Wolf, *Daily Life*, pp. 8-9.

Wolf, *Daily Life*, p. 10.

Wolf, *Daily Life*, p. 10.

Winroth, *Age of the Vikings*, pp. 162-64.

Winroth, *Age of the Vikings*, pp. 162-64.

Winroth, *Age of the Vikings*, pp. 163-64.

Neil Oliver, *The Vikings: A New History* (New York: Pegasus Books LLC, 2013), p. 108.

Winroth, *Age of the Vikings*, p. 123.

John Haywood, *Northmen: The Viking Saga AD 793-1241* (New York: St. Martin's Press, 2015), p. 14.

Wolf, *Daily Life*, p. 24; Graham-Campbell, *Cultural Atlas*, p. 75.

Haywood, *Northmen*, pp. 20-22; Graham-Campbell, *Cultural Atlas*, p. 75.

Haywood, *Northmen*, p. 22.

Graham-Campbell, *Cultural Atlas*, p. 75.

Graham-Campbell, *Cultural Atlas*, p. 79.

[1] Wolf, *Daily Life*, p. 24.

[1] Graham-Campbell, *Cultural Atlas*, p. 78.

[1] Graham-Campbell, *Cultural Atlas*, p. 78.

[1] Hall, *World of the Vikings*, pp. 33, 99.

[1] Hall, *World of the Vikings*, p. 101.

[1] Hall, *World of the Vikings*, p. 101.

[1] Winroth, *Age of the Vikings*, pp. 124-27,

[1] Graham-Campbell, *Cultural Atlas*, p. 78.

[1] Graham-Campbell, *Cultural Atlas*, p. 85.

[1] Hall, *World of the Vikings*, p. 59.

[1] Hall, *World of the Vikings*, p. 60.

[1] Hall, *World of the Vikings*, p. 60. Ribe is a town in Denmark.

[1] Haywood, *Northmen*, pp. 42-3.

[1] Haywood, *Northmen*, p. 45.

[1] Haywood, *Northmen*, pp. 45, 88.

[1] Haywood, *Northmen*, pp. 169-70.

[1] Haywood, *Northmen*, p. 40.

[1] Winroth, *Age of the Vikings*, p. 136.

[1] Winroth, *Age of the Vikings*, pp. 136-39.

[1] Winroth, *Age of the Vikings*, pp. 136-37.

[1] Oliver, *New History*, pp. 99-100.

[1] Hall, *Vikings*, p. 54.

[1] Winroth, *Age of the Vikings*, p. 75.

[1] Haywood, *Northmen*, p. 47.

[1] Haywood, *Northmen*, p. 50.

[1] Oliver, New History, p. 169.

[1] Caroline Taggart, *The Book of English Place Names: How Our Towns and Villages Got Their Names* (n. p.: Ebury Press, 2011), pp. 15, 82, 269.

[1] Graham-Campbell, *Cultural Atlas*, pp. 190-91; Winroth, *Age of the Vikings*, p. 114.

[1] Graham-Campbell, *Cultural Atlas*, pp. 190-91.

[1] Graham-Campbell, *Cultural Atlas*, p. 192; Hall, *Vikings*, p. 97.

[1] Hall, *Vikings*, pp. 150, 152.

[1] Hall, *Vikings,* p. 151.

[1] Hall, *Vikings*, p. 181.

[1] Hall, *Vikings*, p. 160.

[1] Hall, *Vikings*, p. 161.

[1] Ben Waggoner, trans., *The Sagas of Ragnar Lodbrok* (New Haven: The Troth, 2009), p. xiii.

[1] Waggoner, *Sagas of Ragnar Lodbrok*, p. xi.

[1] Waggoner, *Sagas of Ragnar Lodbrok*, p. xiii.

[1] Waggoner, *Sagas of Ragnar Lodbrok*, p. xxiv. The manuscript in question is Copenhagen, Royal Danish Library, MS NkS 1824b 4to.

[1] This manuscript is Copenhagen, Royal Danish Library, MS AM 147 4to. Waggoner, *Sagas of Ragnar Lodbrok*, p. xxiv.

[1] Waggoner, *Sagas of Ragnar Lodbrok*, p. xxv. Waggoner also notes that the *Hauksbók* was broken up into its constituent pieces, and the pieces were rebound and catalogued separately. The portion containing the *Tale of Ragnar's Sons* now resides in the Arnamagnaean Institute at the University of Copenhagan as MS AM 544.

[1] Robert Crawford, *Scotland's Books: A History of Scottish Literature* (Oxford: Oxford University Press, 2009), n. p., accessed through Google Books <http://google.com/books> 23 March 2020.

[1] n. a., "Teutonic Forms," p. 3 (PDF accessed via https://www.jsicmail.ac.uk, 23 March 2020). The PDF appears to cite Turville-Petre, p. xix, as a source for the definition of *háttlausa* but does not give a bibliographical description beyond the author's surname and page number. It is possible that this information was taken from *Scaldic Poetry* by Gabriel Turville-Petre (Oxford: Clarendon Press, 1976), p. xxix, but I do not have access to this volume and so cannot confirm the accuracy of this assumption.

[1] Waggoner, *Sagas of Ragnar Lodbrok*, p. x.

[1] Oliver Elton, trans. *The Nine Books of the Danish History of Saxo Grammaticus*. 2 vols. (London: Norroena Society, [1905]).

[1] Elton, trans., *Saxo Grammaticus*, vol. 2, pp. 544-5.

[1] Elton, trans., *Saxo Grammaticus*, vol. 2, pp. 550 (Charlemagne episode) and 552-4 (Hellespont episode).

[1] Winroth, *Age of the Vikings*, pp. 134-38.

[1] Wolf, *Daily Life*, p. 55.

[1] Wolf, *Daily Life*, p. 55.

[1] Crawford, *Volsungs,* p. xv.

[1] R. Bartlett, "The Viking Hiatus in the Cult of Saints as Seen in the Twelfth Century," in *The Long Twelfth-Century View of the Anglo-Saxon Past*, edited by Martin Brett and David A. Woodman (Abingdon: Routledge, 2016), p. 18. Bartlett cites the F manuscript of the *Chronicle*, f. 54. "Viking Hiatus," n. 16.

[1] Bartlett, "Viking Hiatus," pp. 17-8.

[1] Bartlett, "Viking Hiatus," p. 18.

[1] Waggoner, *Sagas of Ragnar Lodbrok*, pp. xvi-xvii.

[1] Crawford, *Volsungs,* p. xix.

[1] Albert Welles, *The Pedigree and History of the Washington Family* (New York: Society Library, 1879).

[1] Welles, *Washington*, p. iv.

[1] In one medieval version of the saga, Ragnar states that he is fifteen years old in his verse to Thora, but this version does not include Ragnar's sojourn with Lagertha. Because I am including the story about Ragnar meeting and marrying Lagertha prior to his encounter with the dragon, I have changed Ragnar's age to eighteen to take his three years with Lagertha into account.

[1] A kenning for "dragon."

[1] Another kenning for "dragon."

[1] A kenning for "black." This is also a play on the name "Kraka," which itself means "crow."

[1] The original sources are unclear about what the exact nature of Ivar's disability was. In some ways, the descriptions seem to suggest a milder form of brittle bone disease (*osteogenesis imperfecta*), but they could also refer to rickets. Rickets is a childhood ailment that leads to a softening of the bones, which is caused by a lack of vitamin D. Effects of this softening include bow-leggedness and knock knees, which impairs one's ability to walk. Rickets is more common in northern latitudes because of the lack of sunlight during a significant part of the year. It can also be caused by genetic factors or by the mother having a severe vitamin D deficiency during pregnancy.

[1] Kraka/Aslaug's father also had the ability to understand the speech of birds, which he acquired by accidentally tasting some of the dragon Fafnir's blood while roasting its heart for Regin, the blacksmith to whom Sigurd was apprenticed and who was the brother of Fafnir.

[1] "Fafnirsbane" means "Killer of Fafnir."

[1] Although the saga was only written down in Christian times, one wonders whether the pit of snakes was intended to be some kind of reference to the pagan concept either of Hvergelmir or of Nastrandir. The latter was a place in the Norse underworld that was made out of venomous serpents, and the former was a place inhabited by a giant serpent. Nastrandir was the place to which the souls of oathbreakers and murderers were consigned and Hvergelmir the place where the

souls of the most wicked were consumed by the giant serpent. If this coincidence of imagery between pagan beliefs and the saga's text were in fact intended, it may add yet more degradation to the method used for Ragnar's death since it signals that Ella finds him to be not a noble enemy but rather a dishonorable murderer. It is also possible that a link was intended to be made between Ragnar and Gunnar from the *Saga of the Volsungs*, who also meets his end in a pit of snakes.

¹ This is a significantly shortened version of the *Krákumál*, a 29-stave poem purported to be Ragnar's death-song. In fact, the *Krákumál* is a twelfth-century creation, probably written somewhere in the Scottish islands.

¹ Payment of wergild was an important practice in ancient Germanic and Scandinavian societies. The purpose of wergild was to compensate a victim—or the victim's family, if the victim had been killed—for the hurt they had received through the perpetrator's commission of a crime. The amount to be paid varied depending on the nature of the injury and the gender and social status of the parties concerned. Once wergild had been paid, the victim and/or their family had to relinquish any right to exact further payment or vengeance.

¹ Some of the sources I consulted said that "Lundunaborg" was London; others said that it was Lincoln. Neither identification can be historically accurate since both London and Lincoln were founded by the Romans long before the Vikings ever arrived in England. Peter Munch is in the "London" camp in his *Norse Mythology: Legends of Gods and Heroes* (New York: American-Scandinavian Foundation, 1926), p. 251. Katharine F. Boult, on the other hand, claims that Ivar's stronghold was Lincoln. *Asgard & the Norse Heroes* (London: J. M. Dent & Sons, Ltd., [1914]), p. 253.

¹ The medieval sources do not agree on exactly what Ella's torture and death entailed. Some seem to indicate that the image of an eagle was carved into his back, but another version states that the "eagle" was created by cracking open the victim's rib cage from the back and

then splaying his lungs out as though they were wings. Historian Anders Winroth says that the difficulty in translating the original Old Norse has led to other misunderstandings of the "blood eagle." Winroth says that the interpretation in which an eagle is carved into Ella's back with a knife likewise may be a mistranslation, although he finds it grammatically correct, and that it might have been the saga creator's original intent to say that Ella was killed and then his body left as food for birds of prey. *The Age of the Vikings* (Princeton: Princeton University Press, 2014), pp. 36-7.

[1] Quoted in Henry Resnick, "The Hobbit-Forming World of J. R. R. Tolkien," *The Saturday Evening Post* (2 July 1966), p. 94. Tolkien was less sanguine about the Celtic influences on his work and was offended when an early reviewer of *The Silmarillion* said they noticed a Celtic influence. Marjorie J. Burns, *Perilous Realms: Celtic and Norse in Tolkien's Middle-earth* (Toronto: University of Toronto Press, 2005), n.p., accessed via Google Books, 18 March 2020 <http://www.google.com/books>.

[1] Humphrey Carpenter, *Tolkien: A Biography* (Boston: Houghton Mifflin Company, 1977), pp. 22, 35-36.

[1] Carpenter, *Tolkien,* p. 34-5.

[1] Carpenter, *Tolkien*, p. 71.

[1] Carpenter, *Tolkien*, pp. 111, 200.

[1] J. R. R. Tolkien, "On Fairy-Stories," in *Essays Presented to Charles Williams* (London: Oxford University Press, 1947), p. 64.

[1] Jonathan Evans, "The Dragon-Lore of Middle Earth: Tolkien and Old English and Old Norse Tradition," in *J. R. R. Tolkien and His Literary Resonances: Views of Middle Earth*, ed. George Clark and Daniel Timmons (Westport: Greenwood Press, 2000), 21-38.

[1] Evans, "Dragon-Lore," p. 31.

[1] Margaret Schlauch, trans., *The Saga of the Volsungs: The Saga of Ragnar Lodbrok Together with the Lay of Kraka* (New York: The

American Scandinavian Foundation, 1930), p. 96; J. R. R. Tolkien, *The Hobbit* (Boston: Houghton Mifflin Company, 1966), p. 262.

[1] Schlauch, *Volsungs*, p. 95; Tolkien, *Hobbit*, p. 240.

[1] Tolkien, *Hobbit*, p. 261.

[1] Schlauch, *Volsungs*, p. 101.

[1] Schlauch, *Volsungs*, pp. 96-7.

[1] J. R. R. Tolkien, *The Silmarillion*, ed. Christopher Tolkien (Boston: Houghton Mifflin Company, 1977), p. 213-14.

[1] Tolkien, *Silmarillion*, p. 214

[1] Tolkien, *Silmarillion*, p. 223.

[1] Tolkien, *Silmarillion*, p. 225.

[1] Tolkien, *Silmarillion*, p. 225.

[1] Tolkien, *Hobbit*, p. 25.

[1] Tolkien, *Hobbit*, p. 234.

[1] Tolkien, *Hobbit*. p. 235.

[1] Tolkien, *Hobbit*, p. 235.

[1] Schlauch, *Volsungs*, p. 96-9.

The Clash of History and Drama in the History Channel Television Series *Vikings*

The television series *Vikings*, written and produced by Michael Hirst, ran for six seasons and 79 episodes between 2013 and 2019. As of this writing, a ten-episode extension of season six is planned to be released in 2020. Grounded in a great deal of historical research, the series follows the life and deeds of Ragnar Lothbrok (Travis Fimmel), his wife Lagertha (Katheryn Winnick), his brother Rollo (Clive Standen), and other Viking characters living in the Scandinavian village of Kattegat in the late eighth century.

The series has garnered praise for its high production values and strong writing,[cxxvi] but it has also been subject to criticism for its many historical inaccuracies, which likely arise, at least in part, from the screenwriters' need to structure the episodes and the seasons according to the demands of the television drama genre.[cxxvii] The interactions among historicity, historical inaccuracy, newly created fiction, and the text of the *Saga of Ragnar Lothbrok* in *Vikings* is well worth exploring. However, I do not propose to analyze the entire series here; instead, I will focus on just a few points from the first season that demonstrate these kinds of rich interactions.

The underlying inspiration for *Vikings* was the *Saga of Ragnar Lothbrok* and its continuation in the *Tale of Ragnar's Sons*, along with the history of the early Viking Age. Although the series does incorporate some of the details and characters from the saga, it does not follow the saga's plot with any faithfulness. Instead, Ragnar's saga and actual Viking history provide something of a basic framework on which to scaffold the series. This was done in accordance with Hirst's desire to create a viable drama "based on historical research and historical record," not with making a documentary or with directly adapting Ragnar's saga.[cxxviii] Hirst therefore twists and remolds both the saga and Viking history to allow the Ragnar of the series to partake in events that would have happened long before the historical Ragnar's birth and to interact with other persons, both historical and newly fabricated, who either have no connection to the saga or who exist within the saga but have different interactions with Ragnar and some of the other characters.

There are several reasons why it was more fruitful for Hirst to borrow the idea of Ragnar from the saga but not reproduce the saga itself. One has to do with duration: the original saga would not give the creators of the show as much material to work with as creating a new story using the saga as a springboard. Another has to do with the desire for a modicum of historicity: although we might associate the Viking Age with things like dragons, dragons have never existed. Nor have magical cows that frighten away an army of warriors, for that matter. There is a limit to the degree to which one might have a historically informed series and at the same time reproduce the *Saga of Ragnar Lothbrok* as it stands.

However, a more important reason for incorporating plot elements and characters that are ahistorical has to do with story structure and audience expectations. The *Saga of Ragnar Lothbrok*, like most tales of its sort, has an episodic structure, wherein the story is made up of a series of connected scenes, or episodes, that move us from one end of the story to the other. In the case of the *Saga of Ragnar Lothbrok*, these episodes are made of events from Ragnar's life that move him from the point at which he becomes king after the death of his father, through his marriage to Lagertha, to slaying the dragon, and so on, to the end when he is executed at the hands of King Ella. Episodic structure is one valid way of telling a story, but it is not how most modern visual entertainment is composed.

Modern dramas usually have a three-act dramatic structure, which is the format that Western audiences expect from films and television since they believe it to give a satisfying shape to the story being told. In dramatic structure, the first act introduces the protagonist and shows an inciting event that requires the protagonist to do something by introducing a problem that must be solved. The second act contains the "meat" of the story, where the main conflict and any subsidiary conflicts are played out between the protagonist and the other characters. From the inciting event through act 2 and into act 3, the structural principle of rising tension requires the stakes, the action, and the conflict to continue to increase until the final battle (which may or may not involve actual physical combat, depending on the story being told) in act 3.

Once the main conflict of the drama has been resolved, what remains is the denouement (which literally means "untying"), where the story is brought to a close. In the case of an ongoing series that has a larger dramatic arc, the denouement of one episode—from this point onward referring to one broadcast unit of the series—might function as both an ending for that episode itself and a springboard to the next. Episodes that end on cliffhangers lack a denouement entirely since the cliffhanger suspends the story in the middle of the action, leaving the denouement to the episode that concludes the story as a whole.

Some of the historical inaccuracies and departures from the medieval *Saga of Ragnar Lothbrok* in *Vikings* likely are the result of the screenwriters wishing to adhere to the principles underlying dramatic structure, which requires conflict between a clearly defined protagonist and a clearly defined antagonist who move through the story participating in action that conforms to the principle of rising tension. The screenwriters also need to follow the principle referred to as "show, don't tell," wherein important exposition is delivered in ways other than by having the characters' dialogue or a voiceover explain things to the audience. Although "show, don't tell" is also a principle for written things like novels, it is especially important for film and television, which are both visual media.

In the first season of *Vikings*, Ragnar—who here is a farmer and family man living in the village of Kattegat, not the son of a king as in the saga—is working together with his friend, the eccentric shipwright Floki (Gustaf Skarsgård), to create a new kind of ship that will be able to sail the North Atlantic and survive bad weather. Ragnar intends to sail westward to see what he can find because he's tired of going on raids to the east. However, Earl Haraldson (Gabriel Byrne), the local nobleman who holds sway over Kattegat, doesn't want Ragnar to go on this voyage. Haraldson is jealous of Ragnar's enterprising spirit because he sees Ragnar as competition for the loyalties of the men under his jurisdiction.

Ragnar disobeys the earl's direct order not to sail west. Ragnar and Floki, along with Ragnar's brother, Rollo, and other men, sail in Floki's new ship to England. On the journey, they contend with a great storm that might have destroyed other ships, but they weather the storm successfully. Floki is elated that his design works as intended. The Vikings beach their ship on the holy island of Lindisfarne off the coast of England. There they go ashore and raid Lindisfarne's monastery, killing some of the monks and taking others captive as slaves. Among the captives is Athelstan (George Blagden), a young English monk who becomes Ragnar's slave and then his friend.

Although the raid and the trial of Floki's ship design are both successful, all is not well. When the Vikings return home, Earl Haraldson is angry that Ragnar disobeyed him, so he confiscates the treasure that Ragnar and his friends looted from the monastery. The conflict between the earl and Ragnar then drives the arc for the rest of the season, running in parallel both with an important secondary conflict between Ragnar and his brother, Rollo, who is jealous of his brother's leadership, and also with the developing relationship between Ragnar and Athelstan.

In this very brief synopsis of the first two episodes of the first season, we can already see several historical inaccuracies—some of them quite glaring—as well as several departures from the text of the original saga. The first set of inaccuracies concerns elements of Ragnar's forbidden raid. Specifically, these are the idea that Britain was *terra nova* to the Vikings, the idea that the Vikings did not already have ships capable of sailing the North Atlantic even in storms, and the conflict between the date of the actual historical raid on Lindisfarne and the life of the historical Ragnar or Ragnars mentioned in contemporary chronicles.

The historical raid on Lindisfarne happened in 793, while the man or composite character who became the protagonist of the *Saga of Ragnar Lothbrok* was active in the middle of the ninth century. The historical Ragnar likely had not even been born when Lindisfarne was raided, and neither the medieval chronicles nor Ragnar's saga mention any trip to England other than Ragnar's final, fatal attack on Northumbria. It also seems unlikely either that Viking shipbuilding technology was incapable of weathering the North Atlantic until the point at which Lindisfarne was raided or that the Vikings did not already know something about what lay to the west of their native shores before that point.

By incorporating these three concepts into the first part of *Vikings*, Hirst is creating important stakes for Ragnar and the other characters. One raising of the stakes is Ragnar's sailing in an untested ship to unknown lands, which is much more exciting than using technology that is already familiar to sail to a place everyone already knows about. Hirst also uses Ragnar's plans to sail west on a voyage of exploration and plunder in order to introduce the relationship between Ragnar and Floki, which at first centers around the new ship design, and also on the relationship between Ragnar and Rollo, which will be a source of continuing conflict for much of the series that follows. Not only that, but latching onto the famous raid on Lindisfarne puts the fictional raid of *Vikings'* Ragnar on the historical map, as it were, by placing the main character into the center of events that are historically significant and relatively well known. This has the effect of raising the status of the protagonist with respect to this particular element of his adventure.

In addition to twisting historical events to his own ends, Hirst also manipulates historical characters, primarily Ragnar, but also others. For example, a Viking named Rollo did, in fact, exist, although he was of no relation to Ragnar. This Rollo is thought to have participated in the Viking siege of Paris in 885, an event that Hirst also incorporated into his television series beginning in season 3. The historical Rollo was not active only in that one siege; in fact, by 885, he had already been a scourge of northern France for almost a decade, having set up a base in Rouen around 876.[cxxix] Rollo went on to conduct many raids until he finally was defeated in 911 when he attempted to take Chartres. A peace deal with the French king gave Rollo control over the area around Rouen in exchange for the cessation of raids and Rollo's conversion to Christianity.[cxxx] Hirst's Rollo also converts to Christianity as part of a peace deal, but this happens in connection with another raid on England in the season 1 episode "A King's Ransom."

By bringing Rollo into the world of *Vikings*, Hirst creates an important point of conflict for Ragnar. Hirst's Rollo has an uneasy relationship with his brother, teetering between working with him as an ally and working against him as an enemy. The question of whether Rollo will help or hinder (or even kill) Ragnar adds texture to the relationship between these two characters and increases the number of potential storylines and subplots available to the writer.

The final element to be examined is the character of Earl Haraldson and his relationship to Ragnar. Unlike either Ragnar or Rollo, the earl is neither based on a historical figure nor taken from the *Saga of Ragnar Lothbrok*. Instead, Haraldson is a completely fictitious character created by Hirst specifically for this series. Some commentators have found Haraldson's character to be one of the most problematic aspects of the series, not because he is made up out of whole cloth but because of the way he is portrayed and the way he interacts with Ragnar and the other people over whom he rules.

In his 2014 review of the series, George Sim Johnston of the *American Spectator* was especially outraged by the earl's character.[cxxxi] Among the faults found by Johnston was the use of a patronymic ("Haraldson") as though it were a surname or even given name, when in fact Vikings from this period are usually referred to by their given names; for example, Leif Eiriksson is referred to in historical literature as "Leif," not "Eiriksson." But more outrageous to Johnston was the earl's behavior toward Ragnar and the people of Kattegat because Haraldson "rules like a feudal lord, dominating the governing assembly (the 'Thing'), bullying and threatening everyone."[cxxxii]

As Johnston points out in his review, this behavior runs counter to what we know of Viking governance in this period. Feudal, authoritarian modes of governance were not employed until the end of the Viking Age and were motivated in part by the adoption of Christianity by Scandinavian nobles.[cxxxiii] At the beginning of this period, the chieftain's authority derived from his ability to convince warriors to join and follow him. Moreover, the warriors would not have seen the chieftain as being inherently superior to themselves in any way.[cxxxiv]

If Earl Haraldson had been an actual late eighth-century chieftain, he would not have thought to deny Ragnar the opportunity to raid Lindisfarne because Ragnar wouldn't have needed his permission to go in the first place. Nor would Haraldson have confiscated the loot Ragnar and his companions bring back; to do so would have spelled a quick end to an earl's chieftainship and likely to the earl himself, since taking away treasure he had not earned would have been insulting in the extreme. Further, when Ragnar speaks out against Haraldson having condemned a man to be beheaded, Haraldson later tells Ragnar that he has overstepped by speaking against him in public.

Johnston states that the handling of Haraldson's character is "an expression of the tropes to which lazy scriptwriters are prone. Every story has to be about some dynamic young person (who wants freedom) in conflict with a hidebound old conservative, who lives by oppression."[cxxxv] However, what is driving the trope of young explorer vs. old oppressor that is at work here is the need to have a clearly defined antagonist who stands in opposition to the protagonist as part of the basic structure of the work.

Johnston may be correct in assessing Hirst's work as "lazy" on this point since it might well have been possible for Hirst to create a strong foil for Ragnar without running so blatantly afoul of actual Viking philosophies of governance. However, Hirst declined to write his story that way, instead presenting the earl as having strong authority over Ragnar and the others in Kattegat, when in reality early Viking-Age governance was significantly more democratic. For example, at a historical Thing, all free men had the right to speak on whatever item of business was being discussed, and decisions were made by casting lots.[cxxxvi] Behavior such as Haraldson's never would have been tolerated by the real Ragnar or his contemporaries.

Although the many historical inaccuracies in the series may vex historians and reviewers, *Vikings* nevertheless remains a compelling drama that is well written, gorgeously filmed, and full of fine performances from a talented cast of actors. In *Vikings*, we see the embodiment of the Italian proverb "si non è vero, è ben trovato," which loosely translated means, "even if it's not true, it's a good story." *Vikings*, by and large, is not true, in many senses of the word, but like the *Saga of Ragnar Lothbrok* from which the television series takes its inspiration, it nevertheless is a story very well told indeed.

Notes to "The Clash of History and Drama in the History Channel Television Series *Vikings"*

Kirsten Wolf, *Daily Life of the Vikings* (Westport: The Greenwood Press, 2004), p. 22.

[1] Wolf, *Daily Life*, p. 22.

[1] Wolf, *Daily Life*, p. 22.

[1] Richard Hall, *The World of the Vikings* (New York: Thames and Hudson, 2007), pp. 40-43.

[1] Anders Winroth, *The Age of the Vikings* (Princeton: Princeton University Press, 2014), pp. 138-9.

[1] James Graham-Campbell, ed., *Cultural Atlas of the Viking World* (Oxford: Andromeda, 1994), p. 63.

[1] Graham-Campbell, *Cultural Atlas*, pp. 80-83.

[1] Wolf, *Daily Life*, p. 8.

[1] Wolf, *Daily Life*, pp. 10-11.

[1] Wolf, *Daily Life*, pp. 22-24.

[1] Winroth, *Age of the Vikings*, pp. 164-65.

[1] The stories of women warriors in Saxo's history are summarized in Judith Jesch, *Women in the Viking Age* (Woodbridge: The Boydell Press, 1991), pp. 176ff.

[1] Charlotte Hendenstierna-Jonson et al., "A Female Viking Warrior Confirmed by Genomics," *American Journal of Physical Anthropology* 164/4 (2017): 853-60.

[1] Hendenstierna-Jonson et al., "Female Viking Warrior," p. 855.

[1] Hendenstierna-Jonson et al., "Female Viking Warrior," p. 855-57.

[1] Hall, *World of the Vikings*, p. 34.

[1] Jesch, *Women in the Viking Age*, pp. 183-85.

[1] Wolf, *Daily Life*, p. 13.

[1] Wolf, *Daily Life*, pp. 8-9.

[1] Wolf, *Daily Life*, p. 10.

[1] Wolf, *Daily Life*, p. 10.

[1] Winroth, *Age of the Vikings*, pp. 162-64.

[1] Winroth, *Age of the Vikings*, pp. 162-64.

[1] Winroth, *Age of the Vikings*, pp. 163-64.

[1] Neil Oliver, *The Vikings: A New History* (New York: Pegasus Books LLC, 2013), p. 108.

[1] Winroth, *Age of the Vikings*, p. 123.

[1] John Haywood, *Northmen: The Viking Saga AD 793-1241* (New York: St. Martin's Press, 2015), p. 14.

[1] Wolf, *Daily Life*, p. 24; Graham-Campbell, *Cultural Atlas*, p. 75.

[1] Haywood, *Northmen*, pp. 20-22; Graham-Campell, *Cultural Atlas*, p. 75.

[1] Haywood, *Northmen*, p. 22.

[1] Graham-Campbell, *Cultural Atlas*, p. 75.

[1] Graham-Campbell, *Cultural Atlas*, p. 79.

[1] Wolf, *Daily Life*, p. 24.

[1] Graham-Campbell, *Cultural Atlas*, p. 78.

[1] Graham-Campbell, *Cultural Atlas*, p. 78.

[1] Hall, *World of the Vikings*, pp. 33, 99.

[1] Hall, *World of the Vikings*, p. 101.

[1] Hall, *World of the Vikings*, p. 101.

[1] Winroth, *Age of the Vikings*, pp. 124-27,

[1] Graham-Campbell, *Cultural Atlas*, p. 78.

[1] Graham-Campbell, *Cultural Atlas*, p. 85.

[1] Hall, *World of the Vikings*, p. 59.

[1] Hall, *World of the Vikings*, p. 60.

[1] Hall, *World of the Vikings*, p. 60. Ribe is a town in Denmark.

[1] Haywood, *Northmen*, pp. 42-3.

[1] Haywood, *Northmen*, p. 45.

[1] Haywood, *Northmen*, pp. 45, 88.

[1] Haywood, *Northmen*, pp. 169-70.

[1] Haywood, *Northmen*, p. 40.

[1] Winroth, *Age of the Vikings*, p. 136.

[1] Winroth, *Age of the Vikings*, pp. 136-39.

[1] Winroth, *Age of the Vikings*, pp. 136-37.

[1] Oliver, *New History*, pp. 99-100.

[1] Hall, *Vikings*, p. 54.

[1] Winroth, *Age of the Vikings*, p. 75.

[1] Haywood, *Northmen*, p. 47.

[1] Haywood, *Northmen*, p. 50.

[1] Oliver, New History, p. 169.

[1] Caroline Taggart, *The Book of English Place Names: How Our Towns and Villages Got Their Names* (n. p.: Ebury Press, 2011), pp. 15, 82, 269.

[1] Graham-Campbell, *Cultural Atlas*, pp. 190-91; Winroth, *Age of the Vikings*, p. 114.

[1] Graham-Campbell, *Cultural Atlas*, pp. 190-91.

[1] Graham-Campbell, *Cultural Atlas*, p. 192; Hall, *Vikings*, p. 97.

[1] Hall, *Vikings*, pp. 150, 152.

[1] Hall, *Vikings,* p. 151.

[1] Hall, *Vikings*, p. 181.

[1] Hall, *Vikings*, p. 160.

[1] Hall, *Vikings*, p. 161.

[1] Ben Waggoner, trans., *The Sagas of Ragnar Lodbrok* (New Haven: The Troth, 2009), p. xiii.

[1] Waggoner, *Sagas of Ragnar Lodbrok*, p. xi.

[1] Waggoner, *Sagas of Ragnar Lodbrok*, p. xiii.

[1] Waggoner, *Sagas of Ragnar Lodbrok*, p. xxiv. The manuscript in question is Copenhagen, Royal Danish Library, MS NkS 1824b 4to.

[1] This manuscript is Copenhagen, Royal Danish Library, MS AM 147 4to. Waggoner, *Sagas of Ragnar Lodbrok*, p. xxiv.

[1] Waggoner, *Sagas of Ragnar Lodbrok*, p. xxv. Waggoner also notes that the *Hauksbók* was broken up into its constituent pieces, and the pieces were rebound and catalogued separately. The portion containing the *Tale of Ragnar's Sons* now resides in the Arnamagnaean Institute at the University of Copenhagan as MS AM 544.

[1] Robert Crawford, *Scotland's Books: A History of Scottish Literature* (Oxford: Oxford University Press, 2009), n. p., accessed through Google Books <http://google.com/books> 23 March 2020.

[1] n. a., "Teutonic Forms," p. 3 (PDF accessed via https://www.jsicmail.ac.uk, 23 March 2020). The PDF appears to cite Turville-Petre, p. xix, as a source for the definition of *háttlausa* but does not give a bibliographical description beyond the author's surname and page number. It is possible that this information was taken from *Scaldic Poetry* by Gabriel Turville-Petre (Oxford: Clarendon Press, 1976), p. xxix, but I do not have access to this volume and so cannot confirm the accuracy of this assumption.

[1] Waggoner, *Sagas of Ragnar Lodbrok*, p. x.

[1] Oliver Elton, trans. *The Nine Books of the Danish History of Saxo Grammaticus.* 2 vols. (London: Norroena Society, [1905]).

[1] Elton, trans., *Saxo Grammaticus*, vol. 2, pp. 544-5.

[1] Elton, trans., *Saxo Grammaticus*, vol. 2, pp. 550 (Charlemagne episode) and 552-4 (Hellespont episode).

[1] Winroth, *Age of the Vikings*, pp. 134-38.

[1] Wolf, *Daily Life*, p. 55.

[1] Wolf, *Daily Life*, p. 55.

[1] Crawford, *Volsungs,* p. xv.

[1] R. Bartlett, "The Viking Hiatus in the Cult of Saints as Seen in the Twelfth Century," in *The Long Twelfth-Century View of the Anglo-Saxon Past*, edited by Martin Brett and David A. Woodman (Abingdon: Routledge, 2016), p. 18. Bartlett cites the F manuscript of the *Chronicle*, f. 54. "Viking Hiatus," n. 16.

[1] Bartlett, "Viking Hiatus," pp. 17-8.

[1] Bartlett, "Viking Hiatus," p. 18.

[1] Waggoner, *Sagas of Ragnar Lodbrok*, pp. xvi-xvii.

[1] Crawford, *Volsungs,* p. xix.

[1] Albert Welles, *The Pedigree and History of the Washington Family* (New York: Society Library, 1879).

[1] Welles, *Washington*, p. iv.

[1] In one medieval version of the saga, Ragnar states that he is fifteen years old in his verse to Thora, but this version does not include Ragnar's sojourn with Lagertha. Because I am including the story about Ragnar meeting and marrying Lagertha prior to his encounter with the dragon, I have changed Ragnar's age to eighteen to take his three years with Lagertha into account.

[1] A kenning for "dragon."

[1] Another kenning for "dragon."

[1] A kenning for "black." This is also a play on the name "Kraka," which itself means "crow."

[1] The original sources are unclear about what the exact nature of Ivar's disability was. In some ways, the descriptions seem to suggest a milder form of brittle bone disease (*osteogenesis imperfecta*), but they could also refer to rickets. Rickets is a childhood ailment that leads to a softening of the bones, which is caused by a lack of vitamin D. Effects of this softening include bow-leggedness and knock knees, which impairs one's ability to walk. Rickets is more common in northern latitudes because of the lack of sunlight during a significant part of the year. It can also be caused by genetic factors or by the mother having a severe vitamin D deficiency during pregnancy.

[1] Kraka/Aslaug's father also had the ability to understand the speech of birds, which he acquired by accidentally tasting some of the dragon Fafnir's blood while roasting its heart for Regin, the blacksmith to whom Sigurd was apprenticed and who was the brother of Fafnir.

[1] "Fafnirsbane" means "Killer of Fafnir."

[1] Although the saga was only written down in Christian times, one wonders whether the pit of snakes was intended to be some kind of reference to the pagan concept either of Hvergelmir or of Nastrandir. The latter was a place in the Norse underworld that was made out of venomous serpents, and the former was a place inhabited by a giant serpent. Nastrandir was the place to which the souls of oathbreakers and murderers were consigned and Hvergelmir the place where the

souls of the most wicked were consumed by the giant serpent. If this coincidence of imagery between pagan beliefs and the saga's text were in fact intended, it may add yet more degradation to the method used for Ragnar's death since it signals that Ella finds him to be not a noble enemy but rather a dishonorable murderer. It is also possible that a link was intended to be made between Ragnar and Gunnar from the *Saga of the Volsungs*, who also meets his end in a pit of snakes.

[1] This is a significantly shortened version of the *Krákumál*, a 29-stave poem purported to be Ragnar's death-song. In fact, the *Krákumál* is a twelfth-century creation, probably written somewhere in the Scottish islands.

[1] Payment of wergild was an important practice in ancient Germanic and Scandinavian societies. The purpose of wergild was to compensate a victim—or the victim's family, if the victim had been killed—for the hurt they had received through the perpetrator's commission of a crime. The amount to be paid varied depending on the nature of the injury and the gender and social status of the parties concerned. Once wergild had been paid, the victim and/or their family had to relinquish any right to exact further payment or vengeance.

[1] Some of the sources I consulted said that "Lundunaborg" was London; others said that it was Lincoln. Neither identification can be historically accurate since both London and Lincoln were founded by the Romans long before the Vikings ever arrived in England. Peter Munch is in the "London" camp in his *Norse Mythology: Legends of Gods and Heroes* (New York: American-Scandinavian Foundation, 1926), p. 251. Katharine F. Boult, on the other hand, claims that Ivar's stronghold was Lincoln. *Asgard & the Norse Heroes* (London: J. M. Dent & Sons, Ltd., [1914]), p. 253.

[1] The medieval sources do not agree on exactly what Ella's torture and death entailed. Some seem to indicate that the image of an eagle was carved into his back, but another version states that the "eagle" was created by cracking open the victim's rib cage from the back and

then splaying his lungs out as though they were wings. Historian Anders Winroth says that the difficulty in translating the original Old Norse has led to other misunderstandings of the "blood eagle." Winroth says that the interpretation in which an eagle is carved into Ella's back with a knife likewise may be a mistranslation, although he finds it grammatically correct, and that it might have been the saga creator's original intent to say that Ella was killed and then his body left as food for birds of prey. *The Age of the Vikings* (Princeton: Princeton University Press, 2014), pp. 36-7.

[1] Quoted in Henry Resnick, "The Hobbit-Forming World of J. R. R. Tolkien," *The Saturday Evening Post* (2 July 1966), p. 94. Tolkien was less sanguine about the Celtic influences on his work and was offended when an early reviewer of *The Silmarillion* said they noticed a Celtic influence. Marjorie J. Burns, *Perilous Realms: Celtic and Norse in Tolkien's Middle-earth* (Toronto: University of Toronto Press, 2005), n.p., accessed via Google Books, 18 March 2020 <http://www.google.com/books>.

[1] Humphrey Carpenter, *Tolkien: A Biography* (Boston: Houghton Mifflin Company, 1977), pp. 22, 35-36.

[1] Carpenter, *Tolkien,* p. 34-5.

[1] Carpenter, *Tolkien,* p. 71.

[1] Carpenter, *Tolkien,* pp. 111, 200.

[1] J. R. R. Tolkien, "On Fairy-Stories," in *Essays Presented to Charles Williams* (London: Oxford University Press, 1947), p. 64.

[1] Jonathan Evans, "The Dragon-Lore of Middle Earth: Tolkien and Old English and Old Norse Tradition," in *J. R. R. Tolkien and His Literary Resonances: Views of Middle Earth*, ed. George Clark and Daniel Timmons (Westport: Greenwood Press, 2000), 21-38.

[1] Evans, "Dragon-Lore," p. 31.

[1] Margaret Schlauch, trans., *The Saga of the Volsungs: The Saga of Ragnar Lodbrok Together with the Lay of Kraka* (New York: The

American Scandinavian Foundation, 1930), p. 96; J. R. R. Tolkien, *The Hobbit* (Boston: Houghton Mifflin Company, 1966), p. 262.

[1] Schlauch, *Volsungs*, p. 95; Tolkien, *Hobbit*, p. 240.

[1] Tolkien, *Hobbit*, p. 261.

[1] Schlauch, *Volsungs*, p. 101.

[1] Schlauch, *Volsungs*, pp. 96-7.

[1] J. R. R. Tolkien, *The Silmarillion*, ed. Christopher Tolkien (Boston: Houghton Mifflin Company, 1977), p. 213-14.

[1] Tolkien, *Silmarillion*, p. 214

[1] Tolkien, *Silmarillion*, p. 223.

[1] Tolkien, *Silmarillion*, p. 225.

[1] Tolkien, *Silmarillion*, p. 225.

[1] Tolkien, *Hobbit*, p. 25.

[1] Tolkien, *Hobbit*, p. 234.

[1] Tolkien, *Hobbit*. p. 235.

[1] Tolkien, *Hobbit*, p. 235.

[1] Schlauch, *Volsungs*, p. 96-9.

[1] See, for example, Phelim O'Neill, "Vikings: Don't Dismiss This Show as Game of Thrones-Lite," *The Guardian* (23 May 2014), <https://www.theguardian.com/tv-and-radio/tvandradioblog/2014/may/23/vikings-review-history-channel-game-of-thrones>, accessed 9 Mar 2020.

[1] See, for example, George Sim Johnston, "The History Channel Gets *Vikings* Precisely Wrong," *The American Spectator* (12 March 2013), <https://spectator.org/33770_history-channel-gets-vikings-precisely-wrong/>, accessed 9 Mar 2020.

[1] Michael Hirst, "Foreword," in *The World of Vikings* by Justin Pollard (San Francisco, Chronicle Books, 2015), p. 5.

[1] John Haywood, *Northmen: The Viking Saga AD 793-1241* (New York: St. Martin's Press, 2015), p. 98.

[1] Haywood, *Northmen*, pp. 99-100.

[1] Johnston, "The History Channel."

[1] Johnston, "The History Channel."

[1] Anders Winroth, *The Age of the Vikings* (Princeton: Princeton University Press, 2014), p. 143.

[1] Winroth, *Age of the Vikings*, p. 136.

[1] Johnston, "The History Channel."

[1] James Graham-Campbell, ed., *Cultural Atlas of the Viking World* (Oxford: Andromeda, 1994), p. 43.

Appendix: The Tale of Sigurd and Brynhild

The Saga of the Volsungs *is the epic tale of several generations of a single family. It was first written down in the thirteenth century, but the story is considerably older. The complete tale is preserved in both the* Poetic Edda *and in another source under the title* Volsungasaga. *The* Prose Edda *also contains a summary of the story.*

The family whose history is related in this saga is named after Volsung, a hero who is descended from the Norse god Odin. The first part of the story tells the story of Volsung's forebears before launching into the tale of his own family and descendants.

Kraka/Aslaug, Ragnar's third wife, is the child of the Volsung Sigurd and the Valkyrie Brynhild. Kraka's/Aslaug's function within Ragnar's story is to elevate Ragnar's status as a hero by linking him to the Volsungs by marriage.

The synopsis below does not cover the complete Saga of the Volsungs. *Instead, it presents only the part having to do with Sigurd and Brynhild, which is the section relevant to Ragnar's saga.*

Sigurd is the son of the hero Sigmund, who in turn is the son of Volsung. Sigurd's foster-father is a smith named Regin, who is tasked with the boy's education. One day, Regin asks Sigurd about his father's treasure and who is guarding it. Sigurd tells Regin that his wealth is guarded by the king. On another day, Regin tells Sigurd to ask the king for a horse; Sigurd does this, and the king agrees to give him one of his own horses.

The next day, Sigurd is walking through the woods on his way to choose a horse when he comes upon an old man. The old man asks Sigurd where he is going. Sigurd tells him he is going to choose a horse and asks advice of the old man. The old man tells Sigurd to drive a herd of horses into a river that is nearby. (The story doesn't explain where the horses come from, but they evidently do not belong to the king.) Sigurd does so, and all the horses swim across except for one grey horse. The old man tells Sigurd to take that horse; he explains that it is descended from Sleipnir, Odin's own horse, and that it has not yet been ridden by anyone. Sigurd calls the horse Grani. The old man tells Sigurd to take good care of the horse so that in time it will become the best steed in the whole world. Then the man disappears; he was really the god Odin.

Sigurd goes back home, where Regin again asks him about his wealth, which Regin seems to think is being unfairly denied to Sigurd. Then Regin tells Sigurd that he knows how Sigurd can get a lot of treasure and fame. Regin suggests that Sigurd kill the dragon Fafnir and take his gold. Sigurd balks at this. Regin taunts him about it, but Sigurd reminds him that he is still very young and can't be expected to go after dragons, no matter his lineage. Regin backs down and offers to tell Sigurd the story of Fafnir, and Sigurd asks him to tell it.

Regin explains how his brother Otr could transform himself into an otter and often went fishing in a place where the dwarf Andvari dwelled in the shape of a pike. One day, Otr catches a salmon, and when he takes it onto the riverbank, he is killed by Loki. Loki skins Otr and brings the pelt to Otr's father, Hreidmar. Hreidmar demands wergild for the murder of his son. Loki goes back to the river and takes Andvari's gold to use as wergild for Otr's death. The treasure includes a beautiful gold ring, which will have an important role to play in the rest of the saga that follows. Andvari puts a curse on the treasure, saying that whoever owns it will die.

Loki delivers the gold to Hreidmar, who is later killed by his son, Fafnir. Fafnir takes the treasure into the wilderness, where he finds a cave. He puts the treasure into the cave and transforms into a dragon. From then on, Fafnir sleeps in the cave on top of his treasure. Regin says that by taking the treasure, Fafnir has deprived him of his rightful inheritance and forced him to go to the king to ask for employment.

After he has heard the tale, Sigurd becomes angry on Regin's behalf and asks the smith to make him a sword because he has now sworn to kill Fafnir. Regin does so, but when Sigurd smites an anvil with it, the sword shatters. The same thing happens to the second sword. Sigurd then goes to his mother and asks for the shards of the sword Gram, which had belonged to his father. Sigurd brings the shards to Regin and has Gram reforged. When Gram has been made whole, Sigurd tries it against the anvil as he had done with the other swords, and this time the anvil is cloven in two.

Regin reminds Sigurd that he promised to slay Fafnir if Regin made him a sword. Sigurd says that he will keep his promise, but not before he avenges his father, who had been killed in a battle against King Lyngvi. Sigurd goes to Lyngvi's country and begins to pillage and burn. Lyngvi comes against Sigurd with his army, which Sigurd defeats with the help of his friends. At the end of the battle, Sigurd kills Lyngvi.

Sigurd then goes home and tells Regin that he will keep his word about Fafnir. Regin tells Sigurd to dig a pit next to the river and wait for Fafnir to pass over it when he goes to get a drink. When Fafnir's belly is over the pit, Sigurd is to stab him in the heart and so kill him. Sigurd tells Regin that he thinks this a bad plan because the dragon's blood will flow into the pit and drown him. Regin taunts Sigurd, saying that he is a coward and no Volsung.

Stung by this, Sigurd resolves to dig the pit and take his chances. While he is digging, Regin runs away and hides. Then an old man walks up and asks what Sigurd is doing. When Sigurd explains his plan, the old man tells him to dig more than one pit so that the blood will go into the others but not into the one Sigurd sits in.

Sigurd finishes the pits and chooses one to wait in. When the dragon goes to the river, it passes over the pit Sigurd is sitting in. Sigurd thrusts his sword up to the hilt into the dragon's armpit. The dragon writhes away in agony. Sigurd jumps out of the pit and gets his sword back, but when he does this, his arms get covered with the dragon's blood.

As the dragon is dying, it asks Sigurd who he is. At first, Sigurd evades the question and calls himself the "Noble Beast," but eventually he tells Fafnir his name and lineage. As Fafnir is dying, he lays a curse on his treasure.

Once Fafnir is dead, Regin returns. He cuts out Fafnir's heart and drinks some of the dragon's blood. Then he hands the heart to Sigurd and asks him to roast it for him, which Sigurd does. When the heart is nearly roasted, Sigurd touches it to see whether it is cooked and burns his finger. He puts his finger in his mouth, and because it has the dragon's blood on it, Sigurd gains the ability to understand the speech of birds. The birds prophesize about Sigurd's future. They say that Regin intends to betray him and that Sigurd should kill him. Regin takes the birds' advice and cuts off Regin's head. Sigurd eats part of the roasted dragon's heart and keeps the rest for later. Then he goes to Fafnir's lair and takes all the treasure. Among the gold, he finds a helm of terror and other enchanted weaponry. Fafnir's gold is as much as two or three horses could carry, but Grani can carry it all by himself, and Sigurd besides.

Sigurd leaves Fafnir's cave. He discovers the sleeping Brynhild, dressed in armor and lying on a rampart of shields. At first, Sigurd thinks Brynhild is a man, but when he removes her helmet, he discovers she is a woman. Sigurd then removes Brynhild's armor, cutting open her chainmail with his sword. Brynhild wakes up and asks whether the man who cut her armor open is Sigurd. Sigurd says yes.

Brynhild explains that she is a Valkyrie who Odin put into an enchanted sleep because she had killed someone Odin didn't want killed. Odin also made it her fate to marry. Brynhild tells Sigurd that she agreed to Odin's terms, but that she will only marry a man who has no fear, and the only man like that is Sigurd son of Sigmund. Sigurd then asks Brynhild to teach him wise things, and she replies with an extended poem about runes and how they can work different kinds of magic. Sigurd answers with a verse of his own, thanking Brynhild. Brynhild then goes on (in prose) to give Sigurd all kinds of good advice. Sigurd is so impressed he proposes to Brynhild, and she accepts.

Sigurd leaves Brynhild and rides to the court of a king named Heimer, who is married to Brynhild's sister. Sigurd is made very welcome. Some time later, Brynhild arrives at Heimer's court and takes up residence in a separate part of the estate. Sigurd sees her one day and his love for her is rekindled. He goes to visit her and tries to convince her to honor the promise they made to one another and marry him, but Brynhild says that they are not fated to marry one another. Brynhild tells Sigurd that he will marry Gudrun, the daughter of King Gjuki. Sigurd insists that he will marry Brynhild and gives her a gold ring as a pledge of his fidelity; the ring is Andvaranaut, the cursed ring from Fafnir's hoard. Brynhild also pledges her troth.

One day, Gudrun comes to visit Brynhild at Heimer's court. Gudrun and Brynhild talk about famous warriors, and Brynhild praises Sigurd and his prowess. Gudrun tells Brynhild about a dream she had, which Brynhild interprets as foretelling the future, saying that Gudrun will marry Sigurd and that many other woes will befall because of it. Gudrun becomes very sad after hearing this.

Sigurd leaves Heimer's court and goes to Gjuki's, where he is made very welcome, and he becomes friends with Gudrun's brothers,

Gunnar and Hogni. Gudrun's mother, Grimhild, wants Sigurd as a husband for her daughter, so she gives Sigurd a drink spiked with a potion that makes him forget Brynhild and then encourages her husband to get Sigurd to marry their daughter. Gjuki agrees, and at a feast after Sigurd drinks the potion, Gjuki offers him Gudrun's hand. Sigurd accepts, and Gunnar and Hogni swear brotherhood to him.

Grimhild then goes to Gunnar and encourages him to seek Brynhild's hand. They go to Brynhild's father, King Budli, and ask whether Gunnar can wed Brynhild. Budli agrees, as long as Brynhild will accept. Sigmund and Gunnar then go to Heimer's estate, where Brynhild is living in a hall that is protected by a wall of flame. When Gunnar cannot ride through the flames, he exchanges shapes with Sigurd. Sigurd rides through the flames in Gunnar's form and woos Brynhild as though he were Gunnar. Brynhild is reluctant to say yes; she is a Valkyrie, after all, and wants to go back to battle. Sigurd, who is wearing Gunnar's body and speaking and acting as though he were Gunnar, reminds her that she said she would marry the man who could ride through the flames, and Brynhild replies that she will keep that promise. Sigurd takes the ring Andvaranaut from Brynhild and gives her another ring from Fafnir's hoard in exchange.

Remaining in Gunnar's form, Sigurd stays with Brynhild for four days, and when they sleep together, he puts a naked sword between them. Sigurd rides back to his friends and changes shapes again with Gunnar. Brynhild goes to Heimer and tells him she is pregnant with a daughter, Aslaug, and makes Heimer Aslaug's foster-father. Brynhild, Gunnar, and Sigurd return to King Budli's court, where Brynhild's marriage to Gunnar is celebrated. During the feast, Sigurd's memory returns, and he realizes what he has done.

Some time after the wedding, Gudrun and Brynhild go down to the river together to swim. Gudrun shows Brynhild the ring Andvaranaut, which Sigurd has given her; Brynhild recognizes the ring but says nothing. Later, Gudrun and Brynhild have an argument over who has the better husband. Gudrun says that she knows about

Sigurd's vows to Brynhild and taunts her with the story of Gunnar and Sigurd changing shapes so that Gunnar might marry Brynhild. Brynhild warns Gudrun that she will pay for her malice and the betrayal Brynhild has suffered at the hands of Gudrun and her family, but she also says that she loves Gunnar and intends to be faithful to him.

Brynhild takes to her bed. When Gunnar asks what is wrong, Brynhild says that she knows about Gunnar's deception and how he changed shapes with Sigurd. She says that she is downcast because she has broken her vow to Sigurd and that she did not marry the man she was supposed to have married. When Brynhild threatens to kill both Sigurd and Gunnar, Hogni has her chained up, but Gunnar lets her go.

After that point, Brynhild goes into mourning. Gudrun tries to cheer her up but fails, as does Gunnar. Hogni tries next, with no result. Gunnar asks Sigurd to visit her, but Sigurd gives no reply. The next day, Sigurd does visit her and tries to cheer her up. Brynhild reproaches him for betraying her. They argue, and Brynhild says that she wishes she could kill Sigurd. Sigurd confesses that he still loves Brynhild deeply and wants her to be his wife. Brynhild says that she will not leave Gunnar. Sigurd protests that he was bewitched when he came to Gjuki's court and that none of the deception was his fault. Brynhild says that she wants neither Sigurd nor Gunnar now.

After Sigurd leaves, Gunnar goes to talk to Brynhild. Brynhild prophesies that because of what happened, one of the three of them will die. Either it will be Brynhild herself, or else it will be Gunnar or Sigurd. Later, Brynhild tells Gunnar that she will go back to Heimer's court and stay there forever if Gunnar doesn't kill Sigurd, but Gunnar can't do that because he has sworn an oath of brotherhood with Sigurd. Gunnar confers with Hogni about what to do. They agree to ask their younger brother, Guttorm, to do the deed since he didn't swear the oath. Their justification for killing Sigurd is that he had sex with Brynhild during the four days he was in Brynhild's home.

Gunnar and Hogni prepare enchanted food and drink to make Guttorm turn violent and want to kill Sigurd. Guttorm goes to Sigurd's chamber and stabs Sigurd while he is sleeping with Gudrun next to him. The blow wakens Sigurd, who takes his sword and flings it at Guttorm as Guttorm runs away. The sword cuts Guttorm in half, killing him. Gudrun wakes up and finds herself covered in Sigurd's blood and Sigurd himself dying. As he is dying, Sigurd tells Gudrun that he had only behaved well toward Gunnar and that Brynhild was behind his murder.

Gunnar goes to Brynhild and offers her wergild for Sigurd's death. Brynhild refuses. She then has all her gold brought to her and made into a big pile. She tells everyone that whoever wants some of her gold can take it. Once this is done, she stabs herself in the armpit and prophesies many woes for Gunnar, Gudrun, and all the family of King Gjuki. Then she asks to be burned on a funeral pyre with Sigurd, with a naked sword between them. Gunnar prepares the pyre as she requested, placing upon it Sigurd's body, the body of his young son (who Brynhild also arranged to be murdered), and the body of Guttorm. Once the pyre is lit and roaring flames, Brynhild walks into the fire and lies down beside Sigurd, where she dies.

Here's another book by Matt Clayton
that you might be interested in

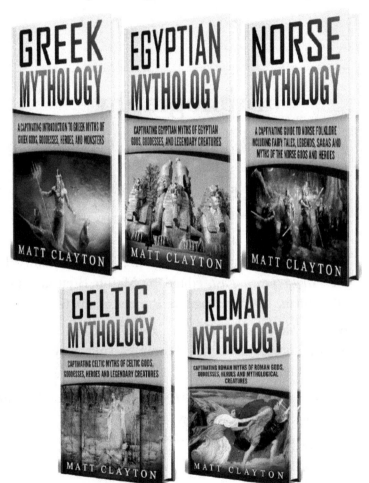

Bibliography

n. a. *Norse Tales of Legends, Gods & Heroes.* Stamford: Longmeadow Press, 1996.

Boult, Katherine F. *Asgard & the Norse Heroes.* London: J. M. Dent & Sons, Ltd., [1914].

Bartlett, R. "The Viking Hiatus in the Cult of Saints as Seen in the Twelfth Century." In *The Long Twelfth-Century View of the Anglo-Saxon Past,* edited by Martin Brett and David A. Woodman, 13-25. Abingdon: Routledge, 2016.

Burns, Marjorie J. *Perilous Realms: Celtic and Norse in Tolkien's Middle-earth.* Toronto: University of Toronto Press, 2005.

Carpenter, Humphrey. *Tolkien: A Biography.* Boston: Houghton Mifflin Company, 1977.

Crawford, Jackson, trans. *The Saga of the Volsungs, with the Saga of Ragnar Lothbrok.* Indianapolis: Hackett Publishing Company, Inc., 2017.

Edminson, John P. *Stories from the Norseland.* Philadelphia: The Penn Publishing Co., 1909.

Elton, Oliver, trans. *The Nine Books of the Danish History of Saxo Grammaticus.* 2 vols. London: Norroena Society, [1905].

Evans, Jonathan. "The Dragon-Lore of Middle Earth: Tolkien and Old English and Old Norse Tradition." In *J. R. R. Tolkien and His Literary Resonances: Views of Middle Earth,* edited by George Clark and Daniel Timmons, 21-38. Westport: Greenwood Press, 2000.

Graham-Campbell, James, ed. *Cultural Atlas of the Viking World.* Oxford: Andromeda, 1994.

Guerber, Helene Adeline. *Legends of the Middle Ages.* New York: American Book Company, 1929.

Hall, Richard. *The World of the Vikings.* New York: Thames and Hudson, 2007.

Haywood, John. Northmen: *The Viking Saga A.D. 793-1241.* New York: Thomas Dunne Books, 2015.

Heaney, Seamus, trans. *Beowulf.* New York: Farrar, Straus & Gerous, 2000.

Hendenstierna-Jonson, Charlotte, et al. "A Female Viking Warrior Confirmed by Genomics." *American Journal of Physical Anthropology* 164/4 (2017): 853-60.

Jesch, Judith. *Women in the Viking Age.* Woodbridge: The Boydell Press, 1991.

Kidder, Daniel P. *Stories of the Norsemen.* Rev. ed. New York: Carlton & Phillips, 1854.

Magnusson, Eirikr, and William M. Morris. *The Volsunga Saga.* London: Norroena Society, 1906.

Mawer, Allen. "Ragnar Lothbrok and His Sons." *The Saga Book of the Viking Club* 6 (1909): 68-89.

Morris, Charles. *Historical Tales: The Romance of Reality.* Vol. 9, *Scandinavian.* Philadelphia: J. B. Lippincott and Company, 1908.

Munch, Peter. *Norse Mythology: Legends of Gods and Heroes*. Trans. Sigurd Bernhard Hustvedt. New York: American-Scandinavian Foundation, 1926.

Oliver, Neil. *The Vikings: A New History*. New York: Pegasus Books LLC, 2013.

Resnick, Henry. "The Hobbit-Forming World of J. R. R. Tolkien." *The Saturday Evening Post* (2 July 1966): 90-94.

Schlauch, Margaret, trans. *The Saga of the Volsungs: The Saga of Ragnar Lodbrok Together with the Lay of Kraka*. New York: The American Scandinavian Foundation, 1930.

Speight, E. E. *Children of Odin*. Rev. ed. London: Horace Marshall & Son, [1903].

St. Clair, Gloriana. "An Overview of the Northern Influences on Tolkien's Works." *Mythlore: A Journal of J. R. R. Tolkien, C. S. Lewis, Charles Williams, and Mythopoeic Literature* 2 (1996): 63-67.

Taggart, Caroline. *The Book of English Place Names: How Our Towns and Villages Got Their Names*. n. p.: Ebury Press, 2011.

Tolkien, J. R. R. *The Silmarillion*. Ed. Christopher Tolkien. Boston: Houghton Mifflin Company, 1977.

——. *Smith of Wootton Major and Farmer Giles of Ham*. n.c.: Ballantine Books, 1972.

——. *The Hobbit*. Boston: Houghton Mifflin Company, 1966.

——. "On Fairy-Stories." In *Essays Presented to Charles Williams*, pp. 38-89. London: Oxford University Press, 1947.

Waggoner, Ben, trans. *The Sagas of Ragnar Lodbrok*. New Haven: The Troth, 2009.

Welles, Albert. *The Pedigree and History of the Washington Family*. New York: Society Library, 1879.

Wheaton, Henry. *History of the Northmen, or Danes and Normans, from the Earliest Times to the Conquest of England.* London: J. Murray, 1831.

Winroth, Anders. *The Age of the Vikings.* Princeton: Princeton University Press, 2014.

Wolf, Kirsten. *Daily Life of the Vikings.* Westport: The Greenwood Press, 2004.

Kirsten Wolf, *Daily Life of the Vikings* (Westport: The Greenwood Press, 2004), p. 22.

[ii] Wolf, *Daily Life*, p. 22.

[iii] Wolf, *Daily Life*, p. 22.

[iv] Richard Hall, *The World of the Vikings* (New York: Thames and Hudson, 2007), pp. 40–43.

[v] Anders Winroth, *The Age of the Vikings* (Princeton: Princeton University Press, 2014), pp. 138–9.

[vi] James Graham-Campbell, ed., *Cultural Atlas of the Viking World* (Oxford: Andromeda, 1994), p. 63.

[vii] Graham-Campbell, *Cultural Atlas*, pp. 80–83.

[viii] Wolf, *Daily Life*, p. 8.

[ix] Wolf, *Daily Life*, pp. 10–11.

[x] Wolf, *Daily Life*, pp. 22–24.

[xi] Winroth, *Age of the Vikings*, pp. 164–65.

[xii] The stories of women warriors in Saxo's history are summarized in Judith Jesch, *Women in the Viking Age* (Woodbridge: The Boydell Press, 1991), pp. 176ff.

[xiii] Charlotte Hendenstierna-Jonson et al., "A Female Viking Warrior Confirmed by Genomics," *American Journal of Physical Anthropology* 164/4 (2017): 853–60.

[xiv] Hendenstierna-Jonson et al., "Female Viking Warrior," p. 855.

[xv] Hendenstierna-Jonson et al., "Female Viking Warrior," p. 855–57.

[xvi] Hall, *World of the Vikings*, p. 34.

[xvii] Jesch, *Women in the Viking Age*, pp. 183–85.

[xviii] Wolf, *Daily Life*, p. 13.

[xix] Wolf, *Daily Life*, pp. 8–9.

[xx] Wolf, *Daily Life*, p. 10.

[xxi] Wolf, *Daily Life*, p. 10.

[xxii] Winroth, *Age of the Vikings*, pp. 162–64.

[xxiii] Winroth, *Age of the Vikings*, pp. 162–64.

[xxiv] Winroth, *Age of the Vikings*, pp. 163–64.

[xxv] Neil Oliver, *The Vikings: A New History* (New York: Pegasus Books LLC, 2013), p. 108.

[xxvi] Winroth, *Age of the Vikings*, p. 123.

[xxvii] John Haywood, *Northmen: The Viking Saga AD 793-1241* (New York: St. Martin's Press, 2015), p. 14.

[xxviii] Wolf, *Daily Life*, p. 24; Graham-Campbell, *Cultural Atlas*, p. 75.

[xxix] Haywood, *Northmen*, pp. 20–22; Graham-Campell, *Cultural Atlas*, p. 75.

[xxx] Haywood, *Northmen*, p. 22.

[xxxi] Graham-Campbell, *Cultural Atlas*, p. 75.

[xxxii] Graham-Campbell, *Cultural Atlas*, p. 79.

[xxxiii] Wolf, *Daily Life*, p. 24.

[xxxiv] Graham-Campbell, *Cultural Atlas*, p. 78.

[xxxv] Graham-Campbell, *Cultural Atlas*, p. 78.

[xxxvi] Hall, *World of the Vikings*, pp. 33, 99.

[xxxvii] Hall, *World of the Vikings*, p. 101.

[xxxviii] Hall, *World of the Vikings*, p. 101.

[xxxix] Winroth, *Age of the Vikings*, pp. 124-27,

[xl] Graham-Campbell, *Cultural Atlas*, p. 78.

[xli] Graham-Campbell, *Cultural Atlas*, p. 85.

[xlii] Hall, *World of the Vikings*, p. 59.

[xliii] Hall, *World of the Vikings*, p. 60.

[xliv] Hall, *World of the Vikings*, p. 60. Ribe is a town in Denmark.

[xlv] Haywood, *Northmen*, pp. 42-3.

[xlvi] Haywood, *Northmen*, p. 45.

[xlvii] Haywood, *Northmen*, pp. 45, 88.

[xlviii] Haywood, *Northmen*, pp. 169-70.

[xlix] Haywood, *Northmen*, p. 40.

[l] Winroth, *Age of the Vikings*, p. 136.

[li] Winroth, *Age of the Vikings*, pp. 136-39.

[lii] Winroth, *Age of the Vikings*, pp. 136-37.

[liii] Oliver, *New History*, pp. 99-100.

[liv] Hall, *Vikings*, p. 54.

[lv] Winroth, *Age of the Vikings*, p. 75.

[lvi] Haywood, *Northmen*, p. 47.

[lvii] Haywood, *Northmen*, p. 50.

[lviii] Oliver, New History, p. 169.

[lix] Caroline Taggart, *The Book of English Place Names: How Our Towns and Villages Got Their Names* (n. p.: Ebury Press, 2011), pp. 15, 82, 269.

[lx] Graham-Campbell, *Cultural Atlas*, pp. 190-91; Winroth, *Age of the Vikings*, p. 114.

[lxi] Graham-Campbell, *Cultural Atlas*, pp. 190-91.

[lxii] Graham-Campbell, *Cultural Atlas*, p. 192; Hall, *Vikings*, p. 97.

[lxiii] Hall, *Vikings*, pp. 150, 152.

[lxiv] Hall, *Vikings*, p. 151.

[lxv] Hall, *Vikings*, p. 181.

[lxvi] Hall, *Vikings*, p. 160.

[lxvii] Hall, *Vikings*, p. 161.

[lxviii] Ben Waggoner, trans., *The Sagas of Ragnar Lodbrok* (New Haven: The Troth, 2009), p. xiii.

[lxix] Waggoner, *Sagas of Ragnar Lodbrok*, p. xi.

[lxx] Waggoner, *Sagas of Ragnar Lodbrok*, p. xiii.

[lxxi] Waggoner, *Sagas of Ragnar Lodbrok*, p. xxiv. The manuscript in question is Copenhagen, Royal Danish Library, MS NkS 1824b 4to.

[lxxii] This manuscript is Copenhagen, Royal Danish Library, MS AM 147 4to. Waggoner, *Sagas of Ragnar Lodbrok*, p. xxiv.

[lxiii] Waggoner, *Sagas of Ragnar Lodbrok*, p. xxv. Waggoner also notes that the *Hauksbók* was broken up into its constituent pieces, and the pieces were rebound and catalogued separately. The portion containing the *Tale of Ragnar's Sons* now resides in the Arnamagnaean Institute at the University of Copenhagan as MS AM 544.

[lxiv] Robert Crawford, *Scotland's Books: A History of Scottish Literature* (Oxford: Oxford University Press, 2009), n. p., accessed through Google Books <http://google.com/books> 23 March 2020.

[lxv] n. a., "Teutonic Forms," p. 3 (PDF accessed via https://www.jsicmail.ac.uk, 23 March 2020). The PDF appears to cite Turville-Petre, p. xix, as a source for the definition of *háttlausa* but does not give a bibliographical description beyond the author's surname and page number. It is possible that this information was taken from *Scaldic Poetry* by Gabriel Turville-Petre (Oxford: Clarendon Press, 1976), p. xxix, but I do not have access to this volume and so cannot confirm the accuracy of this assumption.

[lxvi] Waggoner, *Sagas of Ragnar Lodbrok*, p. x.

[lxvii] Oliver Elton, trans. *The Nine Books of the Danish History of Saxo Grammaticus.* 2 vols. (London: Norroena Society, [1905]).

[lxviii] Elton, trans., *Saxo Grammaticus*, vol. 2, pp. 544–5.

[lxix] Elton, trans., *Saxo Grammaticus*, vol. 2, pp. 550 (Charlemagne episode) and 552–4 (Hellespont episode).

[lxx] Winroth, *Age of the Vikings*, pp. 134–38.

[lxxi] Wolf, *Daily Life*, p. 55.

[lxxii] Wolf, *Daily Life*, p. 55.

[lxxiii] Crawford, *Volsungs,* p. xv.

[lxxiv] R. Bartlett, "The Viking Hiatus in the Cult of Saints as Seen in the Twelfth Century," in *The Long Twelfth-Century View of the Anglo-Saxon Past*, edited by Martin Brett and David A. Woodman (Abingdon: Routledge, 2016), p. 18. Bartlett cites the F manuscript of the *Chronicle*, f. 54. "Viking Hiatus," n. 16.

[lxxv] Bartlett, "Viking Hiatus," pp. 17–8.

[lxxvi] Bartlett, "Viking Hiatus," p. 18.

[lxxvii] Waggoner, *Sagas of Ragnar Lodbrok*, pp. xvi–xvii.

[lxxviii] Crawford, *Volsungs,* p. xix.

[lxxix] Albert Welles, *The Pedigree and History of the Washington Family* (New York: Society Library, 1879).

[xc] Welles, *Washington*, p. iv.

[xci] In one medieval version of the saga, Ragnar states that he is fifteen years old in his verse to Thora, but this version does not include Ragnar's sojourn with Lagertha. Because I am including the story about Ragnar meeting and marrying Lagertha prior to his encounter with the dragon, I have changed Ragnar's age to eighteen to take his three years with Lagertha into account.

[xcii] A kenning for "dragon."

[xciii] Another kenning for "dragon."

[xciv] A kenning for "black." This is also a play on the name "Kraka," which itself means "crow."

[xcv] The original sources are unclear about what the exact nature of Ivar's disability was. In some ways, the descriptions seem to suggest a milder form of brittle bone disease (*osteogenesis imperfecta*), but they could also refer to rickets. Rickets is a childhood ailment that leads to a softening of the bones, which is caused by a lack of vitamin D. Effects of this softening include bow-leggedness and knock knees, which impairs one's ability to walk. Rickets is more common in northern latitudes because of the lack of sunlight during a significant part of the year. It can also be caused by genetic factors or by the mother having a severe vitamin D deficiency during pregnancy.

[xcvi] Kraka/Aslaug's father also had the ability to understand the speech of birds, which he acquired by accidentally tasting some of the dragon Fafnir's blood while roasting its heart for Regin, the blacksmith to whom Sigurd was apprenticed and who was the brother of Fafnir.

[xcvii] "Fafnirsbane" means "Killer of Fafnir."

[xcviii] Although the saga was only written down in Christian times, one wonders whether the pit of snakes was intended to be some kind of reference to the pagan concept either of Hvergelmir or of Nastrandir. The latter was a place in the Norse underworld that was made out of venomous serpents, and the former was a place inhabited by a giant serpent. Nastrandir was the place to which the souls of oathbreakers and murderers were consigned and Hvergelmir the place where the souls of the most wicked were consumed by the giant serpent. If this coincidence of imagery between pagan beliefs and the saga's text were in fact intended, it may add yet more degradation to the method used for Ragnar's death since it signals that Ella finds him to be not a noble enemy but rather a dishonorable murderer. It is also possible that a link was intended to be made between Ragnar and Gunnar from the *Saga of the Volsungs*, who also meets his end in a pit of snakes.

[xcix] This is a significantly shortened version of the *Krákumál*, a 29-stave poem purported to be Ragnar's death-song. In fact, the *Krákumál* is a twelfth-century creation, probably written somewhere in the Scottish islands.

[c] Payment of wergild was an important practice in ancient Germanic and Scandinavian societies. The purpose of wergild was to compensate a victim—or the victim's family, if the victim had been killed—for the hurt they had received through the perpetrator's commission of a crime. The amount to be paid varied depending on the nature of the injury and the gender and social status of the parties concerned. Once wergild had been paid, the victim and/or their family had to relinquish any right to exact further payment or vengeance.

[ci] Some of the sources I consulted said that "Lundunaborg" was London; others said that it was Lincoln. Neither identification can be historically accurate since both London and Lincoln were founded by the Romans long before the Vikings ever arrived in England. Peter Munch is in the "London" camp in his *Norse Mythology: Legends of Gods and Heroes* (New York: American-Scandinavian Foundation,

1926), p. 251. Katharine F. Boult, on the other hand, claims that Ivar's stronghold was Lincoln. *Asgard & the Norse Heroes* (London: J. M. Dent & Sons, Ltd., [1914]), p. 253.

[cii] The medieval sources do not agree on exactly what Ella's torture and death entailed. Some seem to indicate that the image of an eagle was carved into his back, but another version states that the "eagle" was created by cracking open the victim's rib cage from the back and then splaying his lungs out as though they were wings. Historian Anders Winroth says that the difficulty in translating the original Old Norse has led to other misunderstandings of the "blood eagle." Winroth says that the interpretation in which an eagle is carved into Ella's back with a knife likewise may be a mistranslation, although he finds it grammatically correct, and that it might have been the saga creator's original intent to say that Ella was killed and then his body left as food for birds of prey. *The Age of the Vikings* (Princeton: Princeton University Press, 2014), pp. 36-7.

[ciii] Quoted in Henry Resnick, "The Hobbit-Forming World of J. R. R. Tolkien," *The Saturday Evening Post* (2 July 1966), p. 94. Tolkien was less sanguine about the Celtic influences on his work and was offended when an early reviewer of *The Silmarillion* said they noticed a Celtic influence. Marjorie J. Burns, *Perilous Realms: Celtic and Norse in Tolkien's Middle-earth* (Toronto: University of Toronto Press, 2005), n.p., accessed via Google Books, 18 March 2020 <http://www.google.com/books>.

[civ] Humphrey Carpenter, *Tolkien: A Biography* (Boston: Houghton Mifflin Company, 1977), pp. 22, 35-36.

[cv] Carpenter, *Tolkien,* p. 34-5.

[cvi] Carpenter, *Tolkien,* p. 71.

[cvii] Carpenter, *Tolkien,* pp. 111, 200.

[cviii] J. R. R. Tolkien, "On Fairy-Stories," in *Essays Presented to Charles Williams* (London: Oxford University Press, 1947), p. 64.

[cix] Jonathan Evans, "The Dragon-Lore of Middle Earth: Tolkien and Old English and Old Norse Tradition," in *J. R. R. Tolkien and His Literary Resonances: Views of Middle Earth*, ed. George Clark and Daniel Timmons (Westport: Greenwood Press, 2000), 21-38.

[cx] Evans, "Dragon-Lore," p. 31.

[cxi] Margaret Schlauch, trans., *The Saga of the Volsungs: The Saga of Ragnar Lodbrok Together with the Lay of Kraka* (New York: The American Scandinavian Foundation, 1930), p. 96; J. R. R. Tolkien, *The Hobbit* (Boston: Houghton Mifflin Company, 1966), p. 262.

[cxii] Schlauch, *Volsungs,* p. 95; Tolkien, *Hobbit,* p. 240.

[cxiii] Tolkien, *Hobbit,* p. 261.

[cxiv] Schlauch, *Volsungs,* p. 101.

[cxv] Schlauch, *Volsungs,* pp. 96-7.

[cxvi] J. R. R. Tolkien, *The Silmarillion,* ed. Christopher Tolkien (Boston: Houghton Mifflin Company, 1977), p. 213-14

[cxvii] Tolkien, *Silmarillion*, p. 214

[cxviii] Tolkien, *Silmarillion*, p. 223.

[cxix] Tolkien, *Silmarillion*, p. 225.

[cxx] Tolkien, *Silmarillion*, p. 225.

[cxxi] Tolkien, *Hobbit*, p. 25.

[cxxii] Tolkien, *Hobbit*, p. 234.

[cxxiii] Tolkien, *Hobbit*. p. 235.

[cxxiv] Tolkien, *Hobbit*, p. 235.

[cxxv] Schlauch, *Volsungs*, p. 96-9.

[cxxvi] See, for example, Phelim O'Neill, "Vikings: Don't Dismiss This Show as Game of Thrones-Lite," *The Guardian* (23 May 2014), <https://www.theguardian.com/tv-and-radio/tvandradioblog/2014/may/23/vikings-review-history-channel-game-of-thrones>, accessed 9 Mar 2020.

[cxxvii] See, for example, George Sim Johnston, "The History Channel Gets *Vikings* Precisely Wrong," *The American Spectator* (12 March 2013), <https://spectator.org/33770_history-channel-gets-vikings-precisely-wrong/>, accessed 9 Mar 2020.

[cxxviii] Michael Hirst, "Foreword," in *The World of Vikings* by Justin Pollard (San Francisco, Chronicle Books, 2015), p. 5.

[cxxix] John Haywood, *Northmen: The Viking Saga AD 793-1241* (New York: St. Martin's Press, 2015), p. 98.

[cxxx] Haywood, *Northmen*, pp. 99-100.

[cxxxi] Johnston, "The History Channel."

[cxxxii] Johnston, "The History Channel."

[cxxxiii] Anders Winroth, *The Age of the Vikings* (Princeton: Princeton University Press, 2014), p. 143.

[cxxxiv] Winroth, *Age of the Vikings*, p. 136.

[cxxxv] Johnston, "The History Channel."

[cxxxvi] James Graham-Campbell, ed., *Cultural Atlas of the Viking World* (Oxford: Andromeda, 1994), p. 43.

CPSIA information can be obtained
at www.ICGtesting.com
Printed in the USA
LVHW011337140121
676458LV00014B/557